TABLE OF CONTENTS

Top 20 Test Taking Tips..4
Preliminary Work and Collection of Taxpayer Data..5
Treatment of Income and Assets..13
Deductions and Credits..48
Other Taxes...65
Completion of the Filing Process...67
Practices and Procedures...72
Ethics..74
Secret Key #1 - Time is Your Greatest Enemy...76
    Pace Yourself..76
Secret Key #2 - Guessing is not Guesswork...77
    Monkeys Take the Test...77
    $5 Challenge...78
Secret Key #3 - Practice Smarter, Not Harder..79
    Success Strategy...79
Secret Key #4 - Prepare, Don't Procrastinate..80
Secret Key #5 - Test Yourself..81
General Strategies...82
How to Overcome Test Anxiety..87
    Lack of Preparation..87
    Physical Signals..88
    Nervousness..88
    Study Steps...90
    Helpful Techniques..91
Special Report: Additional Bonus Material...96

Top 20 Test Taking Tips

1. Carefully follow all the test registration procedures
2. Know the test directions, duration, topics, question types, how many questions
3. Setup a flexible study schedule at least 3-4 weeks before test day
4. Study during the time of day you are most alert, relaxed, and stress free
5. Maximize your learning style; visual learner use visual study aids, auditory learner use auditory study aids
6. Focus on your weakest knowledge base
7. Find a study partner to review with and help clarify questions
8. Practice, practice, practice
9. Get a good night's sleep; don't try to cram the night before the test
10. Eat a well balanced meal
11. Know the exact physical location of the testing site; drive the route to the site prior to test day
12. Bring a set of ear plugs; the testing center could be noisy
13. Wear comfortable, loose fitting, layered clothing to the testing center; prepare for it to be either cold or hot during the test
14. Bring at least 2 current forms of ID to the testing center
15. Arrive to the test early; be prepared to wait and be patient
16. Eliminate the obviously wrong answer choices, then guess the first remaining choice
17. Pace yourself; don't rush, but keep working and move on if you get stuck
18. Maintain a positive attitude even if the test is going poorly
19. Keep your first answer unless you are positive it is wrong
20. Check your work, don't make a careless mistake

Preliminary Work and Collection of Taxpayer Data

Personal information required for a tax return

All United States citizens and residents who must file a tax return are required to include certain information. To begin with, the taxpayer must indicate his or her full name. If the taxpayer is married and filing jointly, he or she must also include the name of his or her spouse. Either the name of the husband or wife may appear first on the tax return. If the name of the taxpayer has changed because of a marriage or divorce within the past year, this adjustment should be reported to the Social Security Administration before the return is filed. The taxpayer must also include his or her address, whether it is a street address or a post office box number. Taxpayers who live outside the United States may indicate a foreign address. There is a special Form 8822, Change of Address, for taxpayers who are planning to move sometime after filing the return. Completion of this form will ensure that refunds and other documentation are sent to the right address.

Tax returns include an optional space where the client may indicate his or her phone number. This information is not necessary, but giving it can help accelerate the processing of the return. The tax return should also include the tax identification number, which in most cases is the taxpayer's Social Security number. If the taxpayer is married and filing jointly, the return must also include the Social Security number of his or her spouse. Taxpayers who are not U.S. citizens or who do not have a Social Security number should include their individual taxpayer identification number. This information can be obtained through Form W-7, *Application for IRS Individual Taxpayer Identification Number*. The tax preparer will also need to obtain the taxpayer's date of birth and any information about disabilities. Information about date of birth or disability is not required for the forms, but it determines eligibility for certain deductions and exemptions.

Gross income

<u>Minimum amounts for single people and married people filing jointly in 2015</u>
For the purposes of tax returns, gross income is defined as all of the taxpayer's income that is not exempt from taxes. This includes income that is obtained from places other than the United States. The portion of Social Security benefits that is subject to taxation is considered gross income. In 2015, single individuals under the age of 65 were required to submit a tax return if they had a gross income of at least $10,300. Individuals who were 65 or older and wished to file singly were required to file if they had at least $11,700 of gross income. For married couples filing jointly in which both spouses were under 65, the minimum gross income was $20,600. If one spouse was 65 or older, the minimum was $21,500, and if both spouses were 65 or older, the minimum gross income was $22,700.

<u>Minimum amount for married individuals filing separately, heads of household, and qualifying widow(er)s with a dependent child in 2015</u>
For all married people filing separately, minimum gross income was $4,000. Any individual under the age of 65 who wished to file as a head of household was required to file if his or her gross income was greater than $13,250. Heads of household aged 65 or older were

required to file if their gross income was $14,800 or greater. Finally, qualifying widows and widowers under the age of 65 and with a dependent child were required to file a return if their gross income was greater than $16,600. Qualifying widows and widowers aged 65 or older were required to file a tax return if their gross income was greater than $17,850. Remember that any person whose birthday falls on January 1 is considered to have attained the next year of age in the previous year, so individuals who turned 65 on January 1, 2016, are considered to have been 65 in 2015.

Miscellaneous situations that require filing a tax return

Individuals must file a tax return if they meet the minimum gross income requirement, but there are some other scenarios that necessitate the filing of a tax return as well. For instance, a person must file a tax return if he or she received wages of more than $108 from a church or religious organization that itself is not required to pay employer Social Security and Medicare taxes. A person must also file a tax return if he or she is defined as self-employed and has net earnings from this self-employment equal to or greater than $400. An individual may also be required to file a tax return if he or she owes money related to employment taxes for household employees, the alternative minimum tax, or taxes on individual retirement or similar accounts. Individuals are required to file a tax return if they have previously received the first-time homebuyer credit. Also, individuals may be required to pay taxes on a health savings account. Finally, individuals may be required to file a tax return if they have earned tips that have not been reported to their employer, and therefore have not been subject to Social Security and Medicare taxes.

Earned income and unearned income

The necessity of filing a tax return often depends on the individual's amount of earned or unearned income. These values are especially important for determining whether a person needs to file as a dependent. In taxation, earned income is defined as income obtained from work. Some of the most common examples of earned income are salaries, earnings from self-employment, wages, tips, grants, and scholarships that are subject to taxation. Unearned income, on the other hand, is any income that is not the result of work. For instance, a person is not considered to have worked for interest income, so this is considered unearned. Other common examples of unearned income are pensions, annuities, unemployment benefits, ordinary dividends, capital gains distributions, Social Security benefits, and distributions of unearned income from trusts.

Filing deadlines

In most years, income tax returns are due on April 15. However, in years where April 15 is a national holiday or weekend, income tax returns are due on the next business day. Any United States citizen or resident alien is granted an extra two months if he or she is in residence outside of the United States or Puerto Rico on April 15, so long as this person is either in the military or has his or her main place of business outside the United States or Puerto Rico. Similarly, United States military personnel who are serving in a combat zone are given extra time to file a tax return. The amount of extra time is calculated as either 180 days after the last day of service in the combat zone or 180 days after the last day of hospitalization following an injury suffered in combat.

Requesting an extension to the filing deadline

The Internal Revenue Service sometimes grants extensions to the filing deadline, but requests for extension must be made before the filing deadline. Typically, a request triggers a six-month extension, within which the taxpayer will not be charged for filing late. As with the original filing deadline, the October 15 deadline is extended if this day is on a weekend or national holiday. If the taxpayer already owes money for previous tax returns, requesting an extension does not obviate the need to pay this balance immediately. It is a good idea for the taxpayer to pay as much of the expected amount as possible by the original due date, as this will keep any late payment penalty to a minimum. An extension to the filing deadline is obtained with Form 4868, *Application for Automatic Extension of Time to File US Individual Income Tax Return.*

Penalties for late filing and late payment of income taxes

If the taxpayer does not file his or her income tax return by the deadline and has not received an extension, he or she may be subject to a late filing penalty. A tax return is considered to have been filed late if it is not postmarked or electronically filed by midnight of the deadline. In most cases, the penalty for late filing is 5 percent for each month or portion of a month by which the return is late, with the largest possible penalty being 25 percent. Returns that are two or more months late are assessed a minimum penalty of $135. In some cases, a taxpayer will be able to have the late filing penalty waived by demonstrating a reasonable cause for tardiness. Illness and personal hardship are among the common reasons given for late filing. Individuals may also be penalized for late payment of income taxes. In most cases, the late payment penalty is 0.5 percent of the outstanding tax. As with the late filing penalty, this percentage is increased for each month or part of a month in which the tax is not paid, with a maximum penalty of 25 percent.

Form 1040

Individual taxpayers may complete one of three income tax returns: Form 1040, Form 1040EZ, and Form 1040A. There are also special return forms for nonresident aliens and for emendations to an original 1040 form. The tax preparer should select the return form with which the taxpayer can report all relevant income and obtain all possible deductions and credits. Form 1040 is the most basic of the three tax returns. It is also the most detailed, and typically requires the most work. Individuals will select Form 1040 when they need to report business income or itemize deductions. This is also the correct form when the taxpayer has income, deductions, or credits that cannot be listed on the other tax returns.

Form 1040EZ, Income Tax Return for Single and Joint Filers with No Dependents

The simplest tax return is Form 1040EZ, *Income Tax Return for Single and Joint Filers with No Dependents*. This tax return may be used by taxpayers who are under age 65, not blind, and either single or married filing jointly. Any taxpayer who plans to claim a dependent may not use this form. Also, individuals with taxable income of $100,000 or greater must use a different form. On Form 1040EZ, only wages, salary, interest income, and unemployment benefits may be reported. Also, the only credit that may be obtained through this form is the earned income credit. As for deductions, Form 1040EZ only offers the standard deduction, which is automatically calculated.

Form 1040A, United States Individual Income Tax Return

Form 1040A, *United States Individual Income Tax Return*, is less detailed than Form 1040 but more detailed than Form 1040EZ. Taxpayers of any filing status may use Form 1040A. Also, taxpayers who will be claiming dependents are allowed to use this form. However, taxpayers with taxable income of $100,000 or more must use Form 1040. On 1040A, it is possible to report wages, salaries, interest income, ordinary dividends, Social Security benefits, unemployment compensation, annuity income, pension income, and income from individual retirement accounts. The available deductions on this form include those associated with student loan interest, individual retirement accounts, and tuition/fees. It is not possible to itemize deductions on this form. A limited number of credits are available on Form 1040A: these include the earned income credit, the child and dependent care credit, the child tax credit, various educational credits, and the retirement savings contribution credit.

Resident aliens, nonresident aliens, and dual status taxpayers

According to the Internal Revenue Service, a resident alien is a person who is not a citizen of the United States but who has within the last calendar year met either the substantial presence test or the green card test. A person passes the substantial presence test if he or she was physically present for at least 31 days during the last year, was physically present for at least 183 days in the previous three years, and either was physically present for 183 days of the past year or does not have a tax home in another country. A nonresident alien is a person who is not a citizen of the United States and who has not met either of these tests in the calendar year. A dual-status taxpayer is a person who is not a citizen of the United States but who resides here for part of the year.

In the United States, resident aliens typically receive the same tax treatment as citizens. That is, a resident alien may file Form 1040, 1040A, or 1040EZ. Nonresident aliens who are required to report some of their income to the federal government must file either Form 1040NR or Form 1040NR–EZ, *United States Income Tax Return for Certain Nonresident Aliens with No Dependents*. As for dual-status taxpayers, the required tax form is based on the individual's residency status on December 31 of the tax year. If the individual is a United States resident at the end of the year, he or she must file Form 1040 and Form 1040NR or 1040NR–EZ. If the individual is not a United States resident at the end of the year, he or she is allowed to file Form 1040NR or Form 1040NR–EZ.

Filing status

Single
It is very important to the list the appropriate filing status on the tax return. The tax preparer should note that filing status may change from year to year. The taxpayer should file as single if he or she was divorced, unmarried, legally separated, or widowed on the last day of the tax year, and if he or she does not qualify for a different filing status. Widows and widowers are entitled to file as single when their spouse dies before the current tax year and the widow or widower may not file as a head of household or qualifying widow or widower. Any significant change in marital status may affect the ability of an individual to file as single.

Married filing jointly

Taxpayers may register as married filing jointly when both partners in the marriage consent. Because of the favorable tax treatment, married filing jointly is the most popular filing status for married couples. On a married filing jointly return, the couple's aggregated income and deductions are used to compute the overall tax liability. A married couple may file jointly even if one person has accumulated all the income. A married couple may file a joint return even if they maintained separate residences during the tax year or one member of the marriage died and the other did not remarry. However, a married person is not allowed to file a joint return if his or her spouse has filed with the married filing separately status, or if his or her spouse is a nonresident alien or dual-resident alien at any time during the tax year, and does not consent to a joint filing.

In 2014, the IRS began recognizing same sex couples regardless of where they are married. So, even if they do not reside within the state in which they were married they are still required to file either married filing jointly or married filing separately.

Married filing separately

Very few people select the married filing separately status, because it provides the least favorable tax treatment. However, in some cases it may be advantageous for a married person to file separately. For instance, in cases where one partner has low income and higher possible deductions, it may only be possible to reach the income threshold for the deductions by filing separately. Also, couples may elect to file separately to avoid joint and several tax liability from the joint return. In other words, there may be situations in which a married partner does not want to be responsible for the tax burden of his or her spouse. In most cases, however, the married filing separately status results in larger tax payments. This status prohibits taxpayers from claiming many credits, such as the earned income and child and dependent care credits. Also, when a married couple files separately, they must both either itemize deductions or, if one partner wants to use the standard deduction, the other partner will only be allowed to deduct half this amount.

Head of household

In most respects, filing as a head of household provides better tax treatment than the single filing status. For one thing, the head of household return is associated with a higher standard deduction. In order to claim head of household status, the taxpayer must be unmarried or definable as unmarried on the last day of the year. In addition, the taxpayer must pay at least half the cost of maintaining a home over the course of the tax year. This is a requirement for head of household status regardless of whether the home is owned or rented. Finally, in order to claim head of household status the taxpayer must have a qualifying child, parent, or other relative living in his or her home during the tax year.

In order to file as a head of household, a taxpayer must be either single or definable as unmarried on the last day of the tax year. The taxpayer may be defined as unmarried even if he or she is married, so long as he or she meets certain criteria. To begin with, the taxpayer must file a return separate from that of his or her spouse. Second, the taxpayer's spouse may not have lived in his or her home for the last six months of the year. If the reason for the spouse's absence is a special circumstance, the spouse is not considered to have been absent. A married taxpayer may be considered as unmarried only if he or she paid at least half of the cost of maintaining the home during the tax year. Also, it is necessary that the taxpayer's home be the main residence of his or her child (including stepchildren and foster children, but not grandchildren or other relatives). Finally, in order to claim head of household status a married person must be able to claim an exemption for his or her child, or must be prevented from doing so by the concurrent claim of the child's other parent.

Calculation of cost of keeping up a home: In order to file as a head of household, the taxpayer must have paid for a least half the cost of maintaining a home over the tax year. The worksheet provided by the Internal Revenue Service lists the following categories of home maintenance costs: property taxes; mortgage interest expense; rent; utility charges; repairs/maintenance; property insurance; food consumed on the premises; and other household expenses. It is not necessary for the taxpayer to have paid more than half of the cost for each of these items, only for him or her to have paid more than half of the total cost. The taxpayer is not allowed to include any funds received through public assistance programs like Temporary Assistance for Needy Families as his or her payments, though they should be considered in the total cost of maintaining the home.

Requirements for a qualifying child, parent, or other relative: In order to file as a head of household, the taxpayer must have lived with a qualifying child, parent, or other relative in his or her home for at least half the year. In the calculation of residence duration, vacations, school, birth, and death are not counted. One exception is that if the qualifying relative is the taxpayer's parent, it is not necessary for the parents to live in the same house as the taxpayer, so long as the taxpayer pays at least the cost of maintaining the parent's home. A child qualifies for this purpose if he or she is single, even when the taxpayer is not allowed to claim an exemption for the child. If the child is married, he or she may still qualify if an exemption can also be claimed for him or her. A parent qualifies for this purpose is the taxpayer can claim an exemption for him or her. Another relative qualifies for this purpose if he or she lived in the taxpayer's home for at least half the year and an exemption can be claimed for him or her.

Qualifying widow or widower with a dependent child
Individuals who file as a qualifying widow or widower receive the same tax rates and standard deduction as married couples who file jointly. A widow or widower can only file as such for two years after the death of his or her spouse. Also, a widow or widower does not qualify if he or she was not eligible to file a joint return for the tax year in which his or her spouse died. If the widow or widower has remarried, he or she may not use this filing status. In order to file as a qualifying widow or widower with a dependent child, the taxpayer must have a child or stepchild who qualifies. This child must have lived in the taxpayer's home for the entire year, and the taxpayer must have paid at least half of the cost of maintaining the home.

Marital status

The Internal Revenue Service defers to state law in the determination of marital status. In other words, a couple is considered to be legally married for federal tax purposes when the marriage is sanctioned by state law. The following states recognize common-law marriage, which is based on long-term cohabitation: Alabama, Colorado, Iowa, Kansas, Montana, Oklahoma, Rhode Island, South Carolina, Texas, and the District of Columbia. One exception to the federal acceptance of state marriage laws is that the federal government does not recognize same-sex marriages. Same-sex couples may not file joint federal tax returns. Similarly, taxpayers who are formally divorced by December 31 of the tax year may not file a joint return. Couples who are legally separated are considered unmarried by the Internal Revenue Service and may not file a joint return. Annulled marriages are ignored by the federal government, though if either party used a married filing status during the marriage, he or she is responsible for filing amended returns for each related year.

Personal exemptions

An exemption diminishes the amount of taxable income. A taxpayer may claim an exemption for him or herself, his or her spouse, and his or her dependents. Each of these exemptions diminishes taxable income by the same amount, which in 2015 was $4,000. A taxpayer may claim a personal exemption so long as he or she cannot be claimed as a dependent by another taxpayer. Married couples filing jointly may claim two personal exemptions, while married couples filing separately may only claim two if the spouse has zero income, is not filing a return in his or her own right, and cannot be claimed as a dependent. If one member of a married couple dies during the course of the year, the surviving member may claim an exemption for the deceased if the survivor has not remarried by December 31.

Dependency exemptions

A taxpayer may claim dependency exemptions for each of his or her dependents. A child may be claimed if he or she is the taxpayer's son, daughter, foster child, stepchild, sibling, step-sibling, half-sibling, or a descendent of any of these relations. The child must also be no more than 18 at the end of the year, or no more than 23 if he or she is a full-time student. The child must also be younger than the taxpayer, unless the proposed dependent is fully and permanently disabled. Finally, in order to qualify for the dependency exemption, the child must have provided no more than half of his or her own support during the tax year. Student scholarships and Supplemental Security Income are not defined as support provided by the child. The child must also be a U.S. citizen, U.S. national, resident alien, or resident of Canada or Mexico.

Tie-breaker rules
A person may only be claimed as a dependent by one taxpayer, so tie-breaking rules are applied when a person qualifies as a dependent for more than one person. For instance, when parents file separately, the IRS will designate one as the custodial parent if the child spent more nights with him or her during the year. In situations where the child spent the same number of nights with each parent, the exemption is given to the parent with the higher adjusted gross income. When a parent is eligible to receive the dependency exemption but does not claim it, the child may only be claimed by another eligible person if that person has a higher adjusted gross income than the child's parents. If neither of the child's parents can claim the exemption, the exemption may be given to the eligible person with the highest adjusted gross income for the year.

Qualifying relatives
Taxpayers may claim dependency exemptions for other qualifying relatives, who may include family members or people who reside in the taxpayer's household. To be eligible for the dependency exemption, the qualifying relative must have gross income of less than a certain amount ($3,950 in 2015). Scholarship income is sometimes included in this calculation, along with any taxable income. Also, the taxpayer must have provided at least half of the qualifying relative's support during the year. Support is defined as the total cost of the qualifying relative's food, shelter, clothing, education, health care, and other

necessities. Some material purchases, like furniture, may be counted as support, but life insurance premiums and scholarships are not.

Multiple support agreements

The Internal Revenue Service has set up some special guidelines for situations in which several people provide support for a relative, but none of these people provides enough support for the relative to qualify for an exemption. The group of taxpayers who provide support can agree to designate a recipient for the exemption. Remember that only one exemption can be claimed for each qualifying relative. In order to claim a relative under a multiple support agreement, a taxpayer must pay at least 10 percent of that relative's support. Also, the taxpayer claiming the exemption and the other named taxpayers in the multiple support agreement must contribute over half of the relative's support. Claiming this exemption requires the filing of Form 2120, *Multiple Support Declaration*. This agreement must be signed by every taxpayer who is waiving the right to the exemption.

Exemptions related to the children of divorced, unmarried, or separated parents

If the parents of a child are divorced, unmarried, or separated, only one of the parents may claim the child for a dependent exemption. For the purposes of the Internal Revenue Service, the child's custodial parent, and therefore the parent who is entitled to the exemption, is the parent with whom the child spends the most number of nights during the tax year. When parents separate or divorce in the middle of the tax year, the relative number of nights spent with each parent should be counted from the date of the divorce or separation. Nights on which a child should be staying with one parent but instead sleeps at a friend's house, at an organized sleepover, or at camp should be included in that parent's total. It is possible for the custodial parent to waive his or her right to the exemption, so that the other parent may claim it.

Treatment of Income and Assets

Employee compensation

Employee compensation, which is defined as any payment received from an employer for services performed, is fully taxable. Employee compensation may include money, benefits, or other items of value. The most basic way to identify employee compensation is to look at Form W-2. This form helps the tax preparer determine which forms of compensation are taxable. Form W-2, also known as the *Wage and Tax Statement*, lists all of the compensation received by an employee. This will include any benefits that are subject to taxation, such as paid time off, bonuses, and vested stock options. Supplemental wages, which include things like vacations, sick pay, and commissions, are also indicated on Form W-2. Even those supplemental wages that are not distributed in cash form are subject to taxation.

Employer-provided health insurance, retirement plan contributions, and dependent care benefits

When an employer pays for the health insurance of an employee, the employee's spouse, or the employee's dependent, the employee is not taxed for this amount. There is a space on Form W-2 to indicate the amount paid in insurance premiums. The tax treatment is the same for employer contributions to Archer medical savings accounts, health reimbursement arrangements, and health savings accounts. If an employer contributes to an employee's qualified retirement plan, this contribution is not taxed until the employee receives a distribution. However, employers may only contribute a certain amount to each employee's retirement plan. When an employer pays for some of the expense of caring for the employee's dependents, this amount is not counted as the employee's income. For instance, if an employer pays for the employee's child to attend day care, the value of the day care is not considered a part of the employee's income.

Employer-provided group term life insurance, moving expenses, and company vehicle

When an employer provides coverage in a group term life insurance program to employees, the employee is not subject to taxation on the first $50,000 of this coverage. After the first $50,000, the employee will be taxed at a rate corresponding to his or her age. In some cases, an employer will pay for an employee's moving expenses. This money is not subject to taxation if the employee would have been able to deduct the expense had he or she paid it. When an employer gives an employee the use of a company vehicle, the value of this is not taxable to the employee unless he or she uses the vehicle for personal reasons. Transportation to and from work is considered personal use of a vehicle, and is therefore subject to taxation.

Employer-provided transportation, educational assistance, and stock options

When an employer helps pay for an employee's education or training, this amount is not taxable for the employee up to $5,250. Also, in situations where the employer pays for the employee's transportation or parking, up to $230 of this money is not taxable to the employee. If an employee rides his or her bicycle to work, he or she may receive an exclusion of $20 per month for the cost of storage or repair. The tax treatment of stock options depends on whether the options are statutory or nonstatutory. Statutory stock options, otherwise known as incentive stock options, are taxable when they are exercised but not when they are received.

Tip income

The Internal Revenue Service defines a tip as a voluntary payment to an employee by a customer. Tips are always considered taxable income, whether they come in the form of money or other property. On the income tax return, tips are included as a part of wages. Employees are required to keep a daily tally of their tips received and report this amount to their employer. The employer uses this information in the payment of Social Security and FICA taxes. An employee may keep his or her own record of tips, or may fill out Form 4070A, *Employee's Daily Record of Tips*. Employees must record all of the tips received from customers and other employees, as well as the amount of tips paid out to other employees. Mandatory charges for service, such as the standard gratuity assigned to large parties at a restaurant, are counted as wages rather than tips.

Allocated tips

In some cases, an employee will be granted tips by his or her employer. These are known as allocated tips. The allocation of tips is mandatory in some establishments, and tips may also be allocated to employees who report receiving tips less than the worker's share of 8 percent of food and beverage sales. A worker may also receive allocated tips if he or she does not participate in the Attributed Tip Income Program run by the employer. There is a space for indicating the amount of allocated tips on Form W-2. In almost every case, allocated tips are considered to be taxable income, and are subject to Social Security and FICA taxes.

Income of clergy members

According to the Internal Revenue Service, a clergy member is any person who is licensed or ordained by a religious institution, and who performs services in this regard. Clergy members are typically taxed for their income. However, when a member of the clergy is given housing as part of his or her compensation, either the rental value or a designated housing allowance may be excluded from income. The value excluded from income may include the cost of utilities and home furnishings, so long as it is not greater than the fair rental value of the property. Some members of the clergy take a vow of poverty, meaning that they hand all of their income over to the religious institution. In these cases, any payments received by the clergy member are excluded from income if they are turned over to the institution.

Income of military members

In most cases, the income of military members is subject to taxation. For instance, supplemental military leave pay is taxed like normal income. Supplemental military leave pay is the amount paid by the employer to make up the difference between the employee's normal pay and military pay. When an employee is on active duty for a month or more, however, supplementary military leave pay is not subject to FICA taxes. Military members

- 14 -

are taxed on basic pay for active duty and training. They are also taxed on any special pay they receive for hazardous duty, overseas duty, etc. When military members receive funds for the repayment of student loans, this amount is taxable as well. On the other hand, military members are not taxed on combat pay, the basic allowance for housing, and the basic allowance for subsistence. The military member may decide to be taxed on combat pay in order to qualify for the earned income credit. Military members are also not taxed on the following allowances: cost of living abroad, variable housing, burial, dislocation, temporary lodging, and moving.

Foreign income of US citizens

Some of the income of a United States citizen or resident alien who works in another country may be excluded from gross income. In the most recent tax year, the maximum foreign earned income exclusion was $92,900. If this exclusion is claimed, the taxpayer is no longer eligible to claim the foreign tax credit on the associated earnings. In order to qualify for the foreign earned income exclusion, the taxpayer must have a qualifying home in a foreign country. Also, the taxpayer must either meet the physical presence or bona fide resident test. The physical presence test is passed if the taxpayer was in a foreign country for 330 full days during the tax year. The bona fide resident test is passed if the taxpayer is an official resident of the foreign country for at least one tax year without interruption.

Income of statutory employees

Whereas most employees are taxed according to common law, so-called statutory employees are taxed according to statutory rules. Some of the most common examples of statutory employees are traveling salespeople, commercial drivers, and full-time life insurance salespeople. There is a space on Form W-2 to indicate that a person is a statutory employee. The earnings of such a person are not taxed as wages, but rather as self-employment income. This is indicated on Schedule C of Form 1040. Statutory employees are allowed to deduct expenses related to their work; these expenses are not considered miscellaneous unreimbursed employee business expenses, and therefore are deductible on Schedule C rather than Schedule A and are not subject to the normal threshold of 2 percent of adjusted gross income. However, statutory employees must pay Social Security and FICA taxes, though they are not required to pay self-employment taxes on their earnings.

Employees and independent contractors

The difference between an employee and an independent contractor has a significant effect on taxation. Employees report their wages on Form W-2, while independent contractors report theirs on Form 1099-MISC. The difference between an employee and an independent contractor also affects FICA withholding, eligibility for employee benefits, and income tax withholding. An employee is defined as any worker who operates under the employer's control, meaning that the employer determines when, where, and how the employee works. Individuals who are classified as employees pay half of their FICA taxes, and are subject to federal and state income tax withholding. An independent contractor, on the other hand, operates outside of the control of the paying party. When an employer pays $600 or more to an independent contractor, this must be reported as nonemployee compensation on Form 1099-MISC. Independent contractors are responsible for paying the entirety of the FICA tax.

In some cases, a business will attempt to classify employees as independent contractors in order to avoid paying more in taxes. A taxpayer who believes he or she should have been classified as an independent contractor may file Form SS-8, *Determination of Worker Status for Purposes of Federal Employment Taxes and Income Tax Withholding*. This form requests that the Internal Revenue Service ascertain the correct classification for the employee. In the meantime, the taxpayer is allowed to file as an independent contractor. If the Internal Revenue Service then determines that the taxpayer should be classified as an employee, the taxpayer may file an amended return and claim a refund of the self-employment tax. Another way to appeal classification as an independent contractor is to treat nonemployee compensation as wages on the income tax return and abstain from paying self-employment tax. If the taxpayer does this, he or she should report FICA taxes for this compensation on Form 8919, *Uncollected Social Security and Medicare Tax on Wages*.

Interest income

For the purposes of taxation, interest is defined as the fee paid by a borrower to a lender for the use of money. Any income over $10 received from interest is reported on Form 1099-INT, *Interest Income*. If the taxpayer receives interest income of less than $10, it can be reported on the 1040 form with the rest of income. Only a few forms of interest income, such as interest from municipal bonds, are exempt from taxation. Also, interest income is rarely subject to withholding. The Internal Revenue Service has established special reporting rules for the interest earned through foreign trusts or on foreign accounts. U.S. citizens and residents must report interest income earned abroad.

Taxable interest

The most common forms of taxable interest are based on certificates of deposit and bank accounts. However, taxpayers must also pay federal income tax on the interest earned from U.S. Treasury bonds, notes, and bills. Taxpayers are not required to pay state or local income tax on this interest. Taxpayers must also pay interest income on dividends from mutual savings banks, credit unions, federal savings and loan associations, and cooperative banks. This could be confusing because the payments are labeled as dividends rather than interest. Taxpayers are required to pay taxes on the interest from federal and state tax refunds (these amounts may accrue interest when they are left unpaid by the taxing authority for a significant amount of time). It is also necessary to pay tax on the interest from pre-paid life insurance premiums and life insurance dividends. Bonds that are traded flat (that is, purchased at a discount because interest has not been paid on them) are subject to taxation for the interest that accrues after the purchase. Finally, when the taxpayer loans money at a rate lower than the applicable federal rate, he or she will be taxed on the income that should have been charged.

Timetable for reporting interest income

Taxpayers are required to report interest income during the tax year when it is received, whether this reception is actual or constructive. Constructive reception of interest income means that the interest could have been received. Therefore, the interest on deferred interest accounts and certificates of deposit is considered taxable in the year of issuance if the term is one year or less. When the term is longer than a year, the interest is reported on a schedule based on the original issue discount rules. If a bank account is frozen, however, the interest cannot be constructively received and is therefore not subject to taxation. The interest that derives from funds in a savings account should be reported in the year in which it is credited.

Original issue discount

Original issue discount is the taxable interest that accrues during the entire life of a debt instrument. Original issue discount is taxable regardless of whether it is paid to the taxpayer. According to the IRS, a debt instrument is considered to have original issue discount when the price for which it is purchased is less than its redemption value at maturity. If the debt instrument does not pay out interest before maturity, and it has a term of at least one year, it probably has original issue discount. The taxpayer will receive a Form 1099-OID, *Original Issue Discount*, when the amount of the original issue discount is $10 or greater. If the original issue discount is less than a quarter of 1 percent of the stated redemption price at maturity multiplied by the number of years to maturity, then the original issue discount is defined as *de minimis*, and is entered as zero. The only exceptions to the tax rules governing the reporting of original issue discount are for U.S. savings bonds, tax-exempt obligations, and debt instruments with a term of one year or less.

Taxable bond interest

A bond is a debt instrument arrangement in which one party lends cash to another in exchange for an obligation to repay the amount plus interest at a later date. Taxpayers must pay federal income taxes on the interest derived from federal and corporate bonds, but not on the interest derived from state and municipal bonds. Conversely, any interest income derived from United States savings bonds is not subject to state and local income taxes. In a typical arrangement, bond interest is paid twice a year (that is, semiannually). When a bond is sold, the seller must pay tax on the interest acquired during the interval from the last scheduled interest payments to the date of sale, while the buyer must pay tax on the interest that accrues between the date of sale and the next scheduled interest payment.

Interest from state and municipal bonds

Any of the interest that a taxpayer receives on debt instruments issued by state or local governments is not subject to federal income tax. Moreover, in some states and municipalities debt instruments are tax-free when they are issued by that state or municipality. Interest income from state and local debt instruments should be reported on the federal tax return. Specifically, tax-exempt interest is to be reported on line 8b of Form 1040. The amount of tax-exempt interest can influence the tax levied on Social Security benefits. The rules for private activity bonds issued between August 7, 1986, and 2009 are unique. The interest on these bonds is not subject to income tax but is considered as income in the calculation of the alternative minimum tax. The interest income obtained from private activity bonds issued after 2010 is subject to federal income tax.

Reporting of interest income

When the taxpayer receives interest income of $10 or more in a tax year, it is reported on Form 1099-INT. All of this interest is also reported on line 8a of Form 1040. If the taxpayer's taxable interest exceeds $1,500, he or she may not use Form 1040-EZ. Instead, the taxpayer must enter the amount of interest on Schedule B and then transpose this total to line 8a. If multiple people share ownership of the account or debt instrument from which interest is derived, then the respective share of interest is divided according to local law. If these people are not married, then the interest should be reported to the person whose name and Social Security number are given on the W9 form used to open the account. This person is known as the nominee. He or she will receive a Form 1099-INT.

Backup withholding

In some situations, the government will require backup withholding to make sure that individuals pay taxes on their interest income. For instance, backup withholding is required when the taxpayer is notified that he or she has given an incorrect tax identification number, or has failed to give a tax identification number at all. Backup withholding is also required when the taxpayer is found to have underreported interest income on previous tax returns. Typically, backup withholding is equal to 28% of the amount of interest paid. The amount of backup withholding, otherwise known as federal income tax withheld, is reported to the taxpayer on Form 1099-INT. Although backup withholding may be required in some situations, it is not voluntary. Taxpayers who have received a large amount of interest income are advised to estimate their taxes so as to ensure that a sufficient amount is paid.

Interest income from foreign bank accounts

In most cases, the interest income derived from foreign bank accounts receives the typical tax treatment. There are some special rules regarding the reporting of such income, however. These rules are known as foreign bank account reporting, or FBAR. For instance, if the interest income derived from a foreign account has been taxed in that country, the taxpayer may be eligible for a foreign tax credit or deduction for foreign taxes. In general, taxpayers who have received interest income from a foreign bank account should indicate as much on Part III of Schedule B of Form 1040, so long as the amount of taxable interest or ordinary dividends was greater than $1,500, the taxpayer has ownership or an interest in a foreign account, or the taxpayer received a distribution, grant, or transfer from a foreign trust. There is also space in Schedule B for the taxpayer to indicate if he or she had an interest in or any other authority over a foreign financial account. The name of the country in question must be indicated unless the taxpayer was an employee of an authorized commercial bank or a domestic corporation whose securities are listed on one of the national securities exchanges of the United States, or unless the total value of the foreign accounts was never greater than $10,000 during the tax year.

Reporting foreign financial accounts

When a taxpayer has qualifying foreign bank or other financial accounts, he or she must file Form TD F 90-22.1, *Report of Foreign Bank and Financial Accounts*. This form is filed with the Department of the Treasury rather than the Internal Revenue Service. In other words, it is not combined with the rest of the income tax return. The report of foreign bank and financial accounts must be received by the Department of the Treasury by June 30 of the next year, or else the taxpayer is subject to significant criminal and/or civil penalties. The Department of the Treasury does not grant extensions for the filing of this form. In addition to filing Form TD F 90-22.1, taxpayers with qualifying foreign financial accounts must indicate in Part III of Schedule B, Form 1040 whether he or she received a distribution from or was otherwise associated with a foreign trust. Taxpayers who were associated with a foreign trust must file Form 3520, *Annual Return to Report Transactions with Foreign Trusts and Receipt of Certain Foreign Gifts*.

Rental income

In most cases, rental income is subject to taxation. However, property owners may be able to deduct some or all of the expenses associated with maintaining the property from the rental income. Taxpayers must report any rental income that is actively or constructively received. Also, taxpayers should include advance rent, which is any rental payment made before it is required. When tenants give a security deposit to the property owner, the amount of the deposit does not need to be included in gross income until it becomes the permanent property of the owner. In other words, if the tenant damages the property and is forced to forfeit the security deposit, the amount of the deposit should be included in the owner's gross income. Any property expenses paid by the tenant should be included in the landlord's gross income, though they may be deductible. In cases where the tenant makes a large payment in exchange for being excused from a lease, the large payment is considered rental income when it is received.

Rental expenses

Property owners are able to deduct many of the expenses associated with renting out their property, unless they use part of the property or do not make a profit on the rental. The costs of maintaining, ensuring, and advertising a rental property are deductible. Also, the owner of a rental property is allowed to deduct depreciation from his or her rental income. Any interest related to the mortgage of a rental property not used by the taxpayer as a personal residence is deductible. Also, any insurance premiums paid on a rental property are deductible in their entirety, in contrast to the insurance premiums paid on a personal residence. If the insurance premiums are prepaid, they are deductible from rental income for the year in which the coverage is provided. If the property owner incurs transportation expenses while collecting rental income or maintaining a rental property, these expenses are deductible.

Depreciation and maintenance expenses for rental properties

Property owners are allowed to deduct depreciation expense from rental income. Of course, the property owner may only deduct the amount of depreciation associated with the portion of property that is rented out. It may be necessary for a property owner who wishes to claim a depreciation deduction to file Form 4562, *Depreciation and Amortization*. There are various acceptable methods of calculating depreciation. The owner of a rental property may also be able to deduct the expenses of maintaining the property. The Internal Revenue Service makes a strict distinction between repair expenses, which are deductible, and improvement expenses, which must be capitalized (added to the basis of the property). For instance, painting a room is considered a repair, while installing new appliances is considered an improvement. The costs of improvement activities may still be recovered by the taxpayer in the future, though this will need to be through deduction of the depreciation rather than the repair expense.

Expenses for rental properties that are either vacant or not rented for a profit

When a rental property is vacant, the property owner may still deduct the expenses of maintaining it, so long as these expenses are associated with preparing or conserving the property for rental or sale. If the property is rented by the property owner, but the owner does not ever receive the rent, the treatment of this value depends on the property owner's tax strategy. If the property owner uses the accrual method, any rent that is not collected is defined as a bad debt, but if the property owner pays his or her taxes on a cash basis, uncollected rent is not deductible. Rental expenses are less often deductible when the property owner charges less than a fair rental price, or when the property owner declares that he or she is not making a profit on the rental. In these cases, rental expenses can only be deducted insofar as there is rental income.

Rental of the taxpayer's personal residence

If the taxpayer rents out his or her home for more than 14 days out of the year, then the rental income is fully taxable. However, the taxpayer may be able to deduct rental expenses from this income. The value of the rental expenses will be prorated according to the respective length of rental and personal use of the property. The amount of the expense associated with personal use is indicated on Schedule A. In no situation may rental expenses be greater than rental income. If the taxpayer rents out his or her home for two weeks or less during the year, all of the related rental income may be excluded. However, in this scenario rental expenses are not deductible. Instead, the taxpayer will be restricted to the deductions associated with homeownership.

Conversion of rental and personal use property

There are special tax rules for properties that are converted from personal use to rental and vice versa. In cases where a property is converted from personal use to rental, the property is subject to the depreciation allowance beginning on the date of conversion. In the year in which the conversion is made, the depreciable basis of the property is either its fair market value or its adjusted depreciable basis at the time of conversion, whichever is smaller. When a rental property is converted into a personal use property, in that tax year it is treated like a sale of the property. The depreciation allowance for this property is calculated by multiplying the applicable depreciation rate for that tax year by the adjusted depreciable basis of the property at the beginning of the year, and then multiplying this product by a fraction representing the portion of the year in which the property was placed in service.

Passive loss limitations

The Internal Revenue Service has set up passive activity loss limitations to keep a taxpayer from deducting losses incurred through activities to which he or she did not actively or materially contribute. Active and material participation are defined explicitly in the Internal Revenue Code. The general rule is that passive losses can only be deducted from passive gains. An example of a passive loss would be money lost by a nonparticipating investor in a housing development. This investor would not be able to deduct the loss from wages or income. If the investor has not received any passive gains, he or she may carry passive losses forward to a subsequent tax year, at which point they may either be deducted from the sale or disposition of the property, or deducted from future passive gains.

Active or passive real estate activities

Most real estate rental activities are classified as passive, and are therefore limited by passive loss rules. The only exception to this is for real estate professionals, who are allowed to classify rental activity as active income. Regardless of how much effort the owner of a rental property extends preparing and maintaining the property, any loss generated by this activity is considered passive. Passive losses may be carried forward, or suspended, to a subsequent tax year, at which point they may be deducted from passive income or income obtained from the sale of the property. In the rare case that the Internal Revenue Service designates rental activity as active participation, the property owner will be allowed to deduct a maximum of $25,000 from passive and non-passive income. In order to claim the active participation exemption, however, the taxpayer must have a modified adjusted gross income (MAGI) of $100,000 or less. If the taxpayer's MAGI is greater, considerably less of the $25,000 allowance is available.

Real estate professional

Taxpayers who are designated as real estate professionals do not have their passive losses limited. The passive losses incurred by a real estate professional are reported on Schedule C. There are two basic criteria for designation as a real estate professional. To begin with, the taxpayer must be occupied in real estate deals for at least 750 hours during the tax year. Second, at least half of the work done by the taxpayer during the tax year must constitute material participation in real estate transactions. For the purposes of designation as a real estate professional, material participation is defined as continuous and significant work. There are seven ways in which a taxpayer can prove material participation: participation for more than 100 hours during the year, if this is equal to the participation of any other partner; participation for any five of the previous 10 tax years; participation for more than 500 hours in the previous tax year; dominant participation in a real estate transaction business; significant participation for more than 500 hours; participation in the performance of personal service for any three of the preceding tax years; or regular, continuous, and substantial participation during the past tax year.

At-risk limitations on losses from real estate activity

Real estate losses are subject to at-risk limitations as well as limitations on passive activity loss. At-risk limitations mean that the taxpayer must have some money in play in the real estate activity at the end of the tax year in order to deduct any losses from the activity. The amount of money defined as being at risk in a property is the total of the adjusted property basis and the amount of cash put into the property. Any money that has been borrowed and put into the property is also considered at risk. However, if the taxpayer is not personally liable for funds that have been devoted to the property, this value is not considered to be at risk. In other words, when the lender's only recourse is to seize part of the property, the funds he or she owes to the taxpayer are not considered to be at risk.

Reporting income and expenses from rental properties

In most cases, the income and expenses derived from rental property are reported on Schedule E of Form 1040. Taxpayers who are involved with multiple properties must list the income and expenses for each of these properties separately. When the taxpayer owns a rental property and provides significant services for the tenant, this is reported as business income and expense on either Schedule C of Form 1040, *Profit or Loss from Business*, or Schedule C-EZ, *Net Profit from Business (Sole Proprietorship)*. If the taxpayer owns a rental property but does not intend to make a profit on it, any income derived from the property is reported on line 21 of Form 1040. Any expenses related to a not-for-profit rental property are listed as miscellaneous itemized deductions on Schedule A. These expenses are subject to the threshold of 2 percent of adjusted gross income. The taxpayer cannot claim that he or she is not renting a property for profit if the rental income exceeds rental expense for three of five years in a row. Taxpayers who are subject to at-risk loss limitations must file Form 6198, and taxpayers who are subject to passive activity loss limitations must file Form 8582.

Dividends

Dividends are cash distributions to an individual from a corporation in which the individual owns stock. Dividends may also be obtained from mutual funds, which are groups of corporate stocks. If the taxpayer receives $10 or more in dividends during the tax year, this will be reported on Form 1099-DIV, *Dividends*. Regardless of whether they received this form, taxpayers are required to report all of the dividends they received during the year. Dividends that are in the form of cash are subject to taxation, though qualified dividends receive special tax treatment. That is, some dividends, such as distributions of capital gains, are taxed less heavily than others. The highest tax rate for qualified dividends is 15 percent. Qualified dividends must be paid by an American corporation or a qualified foreign corporation. Also, in order to qualify for this special tax treatment, the taxpayer must have owned the stock for at least 60 days of the last 121 (90 days of the last 181 for preferred stock) beginning 60 days prior to the first date after the date from which the buyer of the stock was not entitled to a dividend (what is known as the ex-dividend date).

Nonqualified dividends and dividend reinvestments

The first assessment of whether a dividend is qualified is made by the corporation or mutual fund that pays the dividend. This ruling will be indicated on box 1B of Form 1099-DIV. This judgment is provisional, because the corporation or mutual fund company cannot know whether the taxpayer has held the stock long enough for the dividend to qualify. Nonqualified dividends include distributions of capital gains and dividends based on savings banks deposits. If shareholders are given the option to use their dividend to purchase additional stock, the value of this reinvestment is taxed as if the dividend has been received in cash. Even the service charges associated with the reinvestment are taxable. The value of reinvested dividends increases the basis of the shares held by the taxpayer. The taxpayer is considered to have received dividend income when the reinvestment plan offers additional shares at less than fair market value.

Distributions that are not defined as dividends

In some cases, a corporation or mutual fund will make distributions to shareholders even though it has not made any profits. These amounts, which are called non-dividend distributions, are reported in box 3 of Form 1099-DIV. In most cases, non-dividend distributions are not subject to taxation, because they are considered a return of the capital originally invested by the shareholder. If the shareholder receives non-dividend distributions sufficient to reduce his or her basis to zero, any subsequent distributions should be taxed as short-term or long-term capital gains. When a taxpayer receives a non-dividend distribution but is not issued a Form 1099-DIV, the non-dividend distributions should be reported as ordinary income. Such a distribution should not be reported as a capital gain or a reduction in basis.

Dividends paid in stock and liquidating distributions

When a shareholder receives a dividend in the form of stock rather than cash, this dividend is usually not subject to taxation. Furthermore, distributions of stock options (the rights to purchase stock in the future) do not need to be reported on the tax return. The exceptions to these rules are when the shareholder could have opted for cash instead of the stock or stock options, or when some shareholders receive cash distributions while others receive a greater percentage of ownership. If a corporation ceases operations and liquidates its assets, it may make what are known as liquidating distributions to shareholders. These distributions represent a return of capital, and should be reported in either box 8 or box 9 of Form 1099-DIV.

Reporting dividends on the tax return

If the taxpayer receives a dividend of $10 or more during the tax year, this amount should be reported to him or her on Form 1099-DIV. However, taxpayers are responsible for reporting any dividend amount that is subject to taxation. Ordinary dividends of $1,500 or less are indicated on line 9a of Form 1040. Ordinary dividends of greater than $1,500 must be detailed on Form 1040 or 1040 A's Schedule B, *Interest and Ordinary Dividends*. Qualified dividends, on the other hand, are reported on line 9b of Form 1040, and the special tax rate for qualified dividends is calculated with the *Qualified Dividends and Capital Gains* worksheet. Taxpayers who have received capital gains distributions and must report capital gains or losses must fill out Schedule D of Form 1040. Taxpayers who have received capital gains distributions but do not need to report capital gains or losses may enter this information on line 13 of Form 1040.

Schedule for reporting dividends

The Internal Revenue Service requests that taxpayers report dividends for the tax year in which they are actually or constructively received. Constructive reception of the dividend means that the taxpayer has the right to collect the amount, regardless of whether he or she does so. In cases where stock changes ownership after the declaration but before the payment of the dividend, the dividend is paid to the parties who owned the stock on the record date. A dividend from a mutual fund or a real estate investment trust that is received in January should be counted with the previous tax year, if the dividend was declared in one of the last three months of the previous tax year. Taxpayers who receive dividends as a nominee must complete Form 1099-DIV and Form 1096, *Annual Summary and Transmittal of the United States Information Returns*.

Capital gains distributions

The cash amounts paid out by real estate investment trusts and mutual funds are called capital gains distributions. There is a space for reporting the amount of capital gains distributions in box 2-A on Form 1099-DIV. Capital gains distributions are not reported as dividends, but instead are classified as long-term gains, no matter how long the shares have been owned. Capital gains distributions are treated in a manner similar to qualified dividends, meaning that they are subject to a maximum tax rate of 15 percent. Moreover, taxpayers in the 10 percent or 15 percent tax bracket are not required to pay any tax on capital gains distributions. When a mutual fund or real estate investment trust earns capital gains but does not distribute them, these amounts are still subject to taxation as long-term capital gains. However, undistributed capital gains are reported on Form 2439, *Notice to Shareholder of Undistributed Long-Term Capital Gains*, rather than Form 1099-DIV.

Qualified retirement plans

In tax policy, a qualified retirement plan is one that gives a favorable tax treatment. Some common examples of qualified plans include pension plans, simplified employee pensions, 403(b) plans, and 401(k) plans. Individual retirement accounts are not considered qualified retirement plans. Any distribution from a qualified retirement plan is likely to be taxable, though not to the extent that the distribution includes part of the original investment. Tax preparers may determine the extent to which a distribution is subject to taxation by reviewing Form 1099-R, *Distributions from Pensions, Annuities, Retirement or Profit-Sharing Plans, IRAs, Insurance Contracts, etc.* This form indicates the types of distributions that are taxable, as well as whether any distribution penalties or exceptions to a distribution penalty are applicable.

Taxation of periodic and lump-sum payments
Payments received from a qualified retirement plan are subject to full taxation regardless of whether they are received periodically or in a lump sum. However, taxes will not be assessed for the portion of the distribution that represents the original investment (basis). This portion is calculated with the simplified method for any qualified retirement plans that have an annuity starting date after November 18, 1996. The annuity starting date is defined as the later of the date on which the plan's obligation becomes fixed or the first day for which the taxpayer is eligible for annuity payment. According to the simplified method, the taxpayer's original investment is divided by the expected total number of monthly payments. If the payments are to continue for life, then the taxpayer's original investment is divided by a number provided on the Internal Revenue Service's Simplified Method Table.

Tax treatment of non-periodic payments
The Internal Revenue Service defines some payments from a qualified retirement plan as non-periodic, meaning that these payments are not considered part of an annuity. For instance, if the taxpayer withdraws some cash from the retirement plan, or obtained a loan of funds from the plan, these payments are considered non-periodic. Some non-periodic payments are taxed, depending on whether they occurred after the starting date of the annuity. If the taxpayer dies before the original investment in the qualified retirement plan has been recovered, the remainder of the investment may be listed as a miscellaneous itemized deduction on the income tax return for the year of the taxpayer's death. Moreover, the deduction of the balance on a qualified retirement plan is not subject to the floor at 2 percent of adjusted gross income.

Method for calculation: The extent to which a non-periodic payment from a qualified retirement plan is subject to taxation depends on whether it occurred before or after the annuity starting date. If the distribution was made before the annuity starting date, a portion of it can be excluded from gross income because it can be treated as an allocation to the plan. If the distribution was made on or after the annuity starting date, it should be included in gross income. In the event that a taxpayer accidentally contributes too much money to a qualified retirement plan and subsequently receives a corrective distribution, this is not defined by the Internal Revenue Service as a non-periodic distribution. When the taxpayer places more than the annual allowable amount in a tax plan, all of these excess contributions are subject to full taxation.

Tax treatment of lump-sum distributions

If the taxpayer was born before January 2, 1936, he or she is eligible for unique limitations for lump-sum distributions from qualified retirement plans. For instance, the taxpayer may choose to have the distribution designated as a capital gain, and therefore subject to the tax rate of 20 percent. The taxpayer may also choose to have the distribution taxed at the 1986 single rates, with the rate calculated by multiplying one tenth of the distribution for a single tax year by 10. However, taxpayers who select what is known as the 10-year tax option pay the tax only in the year of distribution. A lump-sum distribution is defined as any distribution that includes the entirety of the taxpayer's balance for a certain type of qualified plan. Taxpayers who qualify for the special rules governing lump-sum distributions must fill out Form 4972, *Tax on Lump-Sum Distributions*. If the taxpayer was born after January 2, 1936, lump-sum distributions are taxed in the same manner as other non-periodic payments.

Tax treatment of losses and net unrealized appreciation with regard to lump-sum distributions

If the taxpayer receives less value in a lump-sum distribution from a qualified retirement plan than he or she originally put into the plan, this loss may be indicated on Schedule A. However, any loss that is claimed on a qualified retirement plan is subject to the limitation at 2 percent of adjusted gross income. This loss may be claimed regardless of whether the lump-sum distribution is paid in devalued securities or cash. When the value of employer securities increases during the term of a qualified retirement plan, the net amount of increase (known as net unrealized appreciation) is not taxable until the taxpayer sells the securities. If there are tax benefits to doing so, however, the taxpayer may include net unrealized appreciation in the total amount of taxable income for the year in which the lump-sum distribution is received.

Distributions from traditional IRA accounts

An individual retirement account, commonly known as an IRA, is not classified as a qualified retirement plan. Therefore, these accounts are subject to different rules regarding distributions. One important factor is whether the taxpayer has made nondeductible contributions to the IRA. This is known as increasing the basis of the IRA. Traditional IRAs are deductible, meaning that the taxpayer has already obtained a benefit for his or her contributions in earlier years, and therefore is subject to full taxation on any distributions. These distributions will be reported by the trustee of the IRA on Form 1099-R. The taxpayer will need to indicate these distributions on either Form 1040 or 1040A, as the reception of a distribution from a traditional IRA precludes the filing of Form 1040EZ.

Distributions from a Roth IRA

All of the money that is used to fund a Roth IRA is subject to taxation at the time of funding, so distributions from a Roth IRA are not taxable. Qualified distributions from Roth IRAs are not taxed at all, and nonqualified distributions are only taxed on the portion of the distribution that represents earnings. Again, because the basis was taxed at the time of its original funding, it is not taxed when it is part of a distribution. Taxpayers who receive a qualified Roth IRA distribution must report this information on Form 1040 or 1040EZ, and must also complete Part IV of Form 8606, *Nondeductible IRAs*. Distributions from Roth IRAs are classified as qualified when they are made on or after the taxpayer reaches age 59 1/2, or made because of a disability, or made to a beneficiary after the death of the taxpayer, or part of the first-time homebuyer exception. Also, the distribution must be made after the first five years of the IRA's existence.

Distributions from nondeductible IRAs

Any distribution from a nondeductible IRA is subject to partial taxation. All of the nondeductible contributions and distributions are to be reported on Form 8606, *Nondeductible IRAs (Part I)*. This form includes a system for calculating the respective amounts of each distribution that are subject and not subject to taxation. The basic formula is to divide nondeductible contributions by the total value of all individual retirement accounts, not excluding any sums withdrawn during the tax year. This generates the percentage of the distribution that is free from taxation. This percentage is multiplied by the total amount of withdrawals to determine how much of the distribution is tax-free.

Required minimum distributions from IRAs and common distribution penalties

Once the taxpayer reaches age 70 1/2, he or she must take a minimum annual distribution from his or her IRA. Taxpayers who fail to do so will be penalized half of the required distribution. A taxpayer may wait until April 1 of the following year to take their first required minimum distribution, but if the taxpayer fails to take a required minimum distribution in the year in which he or she turns 70 ½, then he or she must take two distributions during the next year. There are also penalties for people who receive distributions from an IRA before they reach age 59 1/2. These distributions are subject to a 10 percent penalty, unless the taxpayer is disabled, the distribution is devoted to qualified educational expenses or unreimbursed medical expenses amounting to more than 7.5 percent of adjusted gross income, or the distribution is received by the beneficiary of a deceased individual retirement account owner.

Rollovers of retirement plans

When the taxpayer shifts funds from one individual retirement account or retirement plan to another, this is known as a rollover. A direct rollover is a transfer of funds between custodians or plan trustees. If the taxpayer receives a distribution from one retirement plan or IRA and then deposits it into another, this is also considered a rollover. However, direct rollovers are better because they are not subject to the 10 percent penalty or to taxation should they not be reinvested within 60 days of the taxpayer receiving the funds. The following plans are eligible for rollover: 457 plan; 403(b) plan; qualified employee annuity; and qualified employee plan (e.g., 401(k)). Taxpayers are not allowed to roll over required minimum distributions. The rules for rollovers with Roth accounts are slightly different. Taxpayers may only roll over funds from a designated Roth account to a Roth IRA or another designated Roth account. Recently, it became possible to roll over funds from a non-Roth qualified plan to a designated Roth account.

Conversions of individual retirement accounts

Taxpayers are allowed to convert a portion or the entirety of a traditional individual retirement account to a Roth IRA. The taxpayer will be taxed on the value of the amount converted during the tax year. Both 401(k) and 403(b) plans can be converted into designated Roth accounts, so long as the plan allows for these conversions. Such

- 26 -

arrangements are known as in-plan designated Roth IRA accounts. It is important for taxpayers to keep records of their contributions to an individual retirement account. To the extent that contributions are not subject to taxation when they are made, they should be included in income when they are part of an in-plan designated Roth IRA rollover.

Special taxes on excess accumulations, excess contributions, and early distributions

Taxpayers are required to begin receiving a required minimum distribution from qualified plans and individual retirement accounts once they attain age 70 1/2. Those taxpayers who fail to do so are penalized 50 percent of the required minimum distribution. The first required minimum distribution must be taken by April 1 of the year following the year in which the taxpayer reached age 70 1/2. If the taxpayer contributes more than he or she is allowed to during the tax year, the excess contribution is subject to a 6 percent penalty. If the taxpayer receives a distribution from a qualified plan or a traditional IRA before reaching age 59 1/2, the distribution is subject to a 10 percent penalty. Distributions from a Roth IRA that occur within the first five years of the account's existence are subject to a 10 percent penalty as well, though this is only applied to the section of the nonqualified distribution included in income.

Taxation of commercial annuities

A commercial annuity is purchased from an insurance company. It is not a component of a qualified retirement plan. Taxpayers who own commercial annuities may receive part of the contract as an annual annuity payment, with the rest left behind to accumulate with taxes deferred. The respective sizes of each portion are determined with the General Rules, which take into account the expected return from the commercial annuity. To begin with, the tax preparer must determine the total amount of investment in the contract by the taxpayer. This should be equal to the amount paid for the annuity. The amount of investment is then reduced by any refunds, rebates, or dividends related to the premium. The next step is to determine the expected return from the annuity by adding up all the payments that will come out of it in the future. It may be necessary to use the life expectancy tables put forth by the IRS to figure this amount. Finally, the exclusion percentage is calculated by dividing the total investment in the contract by the total expected return.

Taxation of distributions from life insurance

In most cases, the money that is received from a life insurance policy following the death of the insured person is not subject to taxation. For instance, all of the amounts paid for the policy, as well as any premiums paid while the policy was in effect, are excluded from income. When the proceeds of a life insurance policy are paid in installments, a portion of each installment is considered to be taxable interest. The amount of interest in an installment is calculated by dividing the face value of the policy by the number of years in which installments will be received. The quotient is the portion of the distribution that is not subject to taxation. When the proceeds of a life insurance policy are not paid in installments, meaning that they are paid either in a lump sum or in a non-periodic fashion, they are excludable from income insofar as they represent the amounts to be received by the beneficiary upon the death of the insured. The portion of a new lump sum or non-periodic payments that is excludable from income is known as an original death payment.

Tax treatment of scholarship and grant money

Taxpayers who are in pursuit of a degree generally will not have their scholarships or fellowship grants taxed. Of course, the taxpayer must be spending this money on qualified educational expenses, like tuition, fees, and supplies. Room and board at an educational institution is not considered a qualified education expense. Whatever portion of a scholarship or grant that is not spent on a qualified educational expense is subject to taxation. Any scholarships and grants must be reported on line 7 of Form 1040, with the rest of wages. Even scholarships and grants that are subject to taxation are not reported on line 21 along with other income. With regard to educational credits, scholarships that are free from taxation decrease the amount of qualified educational expenses, while scholarships and grants that are subject to taxation do not.

Handling taxable recoveries

If the taxpayer deducted an expense in the previous year and subsequently received a refund recovery, the amount of the refund recovery is defined as income. This is because the deduction reduced taxes in the previous year. Nevertheless, a refund or recovery may be partially or not taxable. The procedure for determining whether a recovery is taxable requires an assessment of the benefit obtained by the taxpayer during the previous tax year. This exercise is completed with IRS Publication 525, *Taxable and Nontaxable Income*, specifically in the worksheet for Recoveries of Itemized Deductions. For example, taxpayers who did not receive any benefit from the original amount of the deduction will not have the recovery taxed. However, if the taxpayer did receive a benefit, the amount of the recovery will be subject to taxation to the same degree.

Alimony payments

Taxpayers are subject to full taxation for alimony payments received, while taxpayers who make alimony payments may deduct these amounts from their adjusted gross income. The reception of alimony payments is reported on line 11 of Form 1040, while the deduction of alimony payments from adjusted gross income is made on line 31a of Form 1040. Remember that alimony is a payment made from one member of a divorced or separated couple to the other. Any alimony payment that qualifies for taxation for the recipient will also qualify as a deduction for the paying spouse. Likewise, if the spouse who makes the alimony payment cannot deduct it from adjusted gross income, the receiving spouse may not be taxed on the payment.

Income from partnerships, limited liability companies, and S corporations

The owners of partnerships, limited liability companies (LLCs), and S corporations report any income or losses from these entities on their personal income tax returns. For taxpayers who only own a share of one of these businesses, the respective portion of income or loss is reported on Schedule K-1, *Partner's Share of Income, Deductions, Credits, etc.* This form is similar to the one issued to the beneficiaries of trusts and estates. However, there are slightly different versions of the form for partners in limited liability companies and S corporations. Schedule K-1 will indicate basic information about the partnership, the partner, and the partner's respective share of current year income, deductions, credits, and other items.

Royalties

When the taxpayer owns an intangible asset, like a patent or copyright, he or she may receive royalty payments from others who make use of the patented or copyrighted item. In most cases, income received from royalties is reported on Schedule E, *Supplemental Income and Loss*. When royalties are reported on this form, passive activity loss rules limit any deductions related to expenses. If the taxpayer actually runs the business that generates the royalties, income is reported on Schedule C, *Profit or Loss from Business (Sole Proprietorship)*. The Internal Revenue Service has a fairly broad definition for running a royalty-generating business; a taxpayer may be considered to operate a business if he or she merely has an interest in a royalty-generating property, or if he or she is currently self-employed in the creative field that generates royalties (e.g., if he or she was a self-employed musician in the current tax year and earns royalties for songs written in previous years).

Social Security benefits

The amount of Social Security income subject to taxation is not dependent on the age of the taxpayer. Taxpayers must report their Social Security benefits on Form SSA-1099, *Social Security Benefits Statement*. The process of determining the taxable portion of Social Security benefits requires the calculation of the net benefits received by the taxpayer. Up to 85 percent of Social Security benefits may be subject to taxation if the taxpayer's income exceeds the base amount for his or her filing status. The base amount consists of half the Social Security benefits, as well as any tax-exempt interest and other taxable income. If the taxpayer is married filing jointly, the income of both partners must be combined even if only one of the partners has received benefits from Social Security.

Social Security benefits

The IRS has established base amounts beyond which Social Security benefits are partially taxable. In 2015, taxpayers who filed as single, head of household, or qualifying widowers were required to pay taxes on some of their Social Security benefits when their income exceeded $25,000. These taxpayers would be required to pay taxes on 85 percent of benefits if their income exceeded $34,000. Taxpayers who are married filing jointly must pay taxes on Social Security benefits if their income exceeds $32,000, and must pay taxes on up to 85 percent if their income exceeds $44,000. Taxpayers who are married filing separately but lived apart from one another for the entire year must pay taxes on some Social Security benefits if their income exceeds $25,000, and must pay the maximum amount if their income exceeds $34,000. Couples who are married and file separately but lived together must automatically pay taxes on 85 percent of Social Security benefits.

When a parent receives Social Security benefits for both him or herself and a child, only the portion of the benefit that is directed to the parent is subject to taxation. The extent to which the rest of the benefit is taxable will depend on the income of the child. If the taxpayer receives benefits from a previous year in a lump sum, these benefits should be included in the calculation of taxable benefits for the current tax year. However, the taxpayer may elect to calculate the tax on these benefits in a different way, meaning that he or she will use the prior year's income. Taxpayers will select this option if their income in previous years was less than the base amounts required to trigger taxation of Social Security benefits. If the taxpayer is living in a foreign country, but is a U.S. citizen, he or she may be taxed on Social Security benefits. However, residents of the following countries will not be taxed on these benefits: Canada, Ireland, Germany, Egypt, Romania, the United Kingdom, or Israel. Residents of Italy who are also citizens of Italy will not be taxed on Social Security benefits.

Railroad retirement benefits

There are special retirement plans for former railroad employees and their beneficiaries. In taxation, the section of tier 1 benefits a railroad employee would have been entitled to receive under the Social Security system is known as the equivalent tier 1 Railroad Retirement Benefit, or the Social Security Equivalent Benefit. These benefits are reported on Form RRB-1099, *Payments by the Railroad Retirement Board*. Social Security Equivalent Benefits receive the same tax treatment as Social Security benefits. If the recipient of these Railroad Retirement Benefits lives in Canada, Ireland, Germany, Egypt, Romania, the United Kingdom, Israel, or Italy, the benefits are subject to withholding at 30 percent unless the taxpayer files Form RRB-1001, *Nonresident Questionnaire*.

Social Security disability benefits

Any disability benefits that are paid by the Social Security Administration are subject to taxation in the same way as other Social Security benefits. However, disability payments made by the Social Security Administration should not be confused with supplemental security income payments, which are funded by a federal income supplement program and are not subject to taxation. If the taxpayer receives a disability payment from his or her insurance company or employer which he or she is required to pay back because of previous Social Security benefits, then the taxpayer is allowed to deduct this repayment. However, this deduction must be itemized unless it is greater than $3,000, in which case the taxpayer may claim it as a credit. If the taxpayer incurs legal fees in the collection of these benefits, then these may be classified as a miscellaneous itemized deduction, though this is subject to the floor at 2 percent of adjusted gross income.

Unemployment compensation

In most cases, unemployment compensation is an insurance benefit paid by the state. However, the Internal Revenue Service also recognizes railroad unemployment benefits and disability benefits as unemployment compensation in some instances. Unemployment compensation is subject to full taxation by the federal government, with no applicable exclusions. However, if the supplemental unemployment benefits come from a fund that is financed by the taxpayer's former company, these are taxable as wages and therefore are eligible for income tax withholding. The taxpayer's unemployment compensation will be reported on Form 1099-G, *Certain Government Payments*. The taxpayer will then include these amounts as gross income on line 19 of Form 1040. By filing Form W-4V, *Voluntary Withholding Request*, the taxpayer can have income tax withheld from unemployment benefits at a static rate of 10 percent.

Income received from court awards and settlements

To the extent that a court award or divorce settlement is a substitute for normal income, it may be subject to taxation. For instance, if the taxpayer files a claim of emotional distress under Title VII of the 1964 Civil Rights Act, any back pay and damages may be taxed as ordinary income. Similarly, full taxation is applied to any damages received in lawsuits involving breach of contract or infringement of a patent or copyright. If a client receives punitive damages, these are almost always subject to taxation unless the damages are associated with a physical injury or wrongful death. Taxpayers must also pay taxes on the interest received from any award or settlement, as well as any compensation they receive for lost profits or wages.

Canceled debt income

If the taxpayer owes money and then has this debt forgiven in part or entirely, the IRS considers this to be income. The most common examples of cancellation of debt income are related to credit cards and student loans. This income is almost always taxable. If the debt is canceled because the taxpayer has abandoned the property that was the security for the loan, or the lender has repossessed or foreclosed on this property, the cancellation is reported on Form 1099-A, *Acquisition or Abandonment of Secured Property*. Property that is repossessed or foreclosed upon is treated as if it had been resold to the lender. If the lender merely cancels the debt, this is reported on Form 1099-C, *Cancellation of Debt*. Cancellation of debt income may be excluded from gross income if the taxpayer is bankrupt or insolvent. Also, up to $2 million of the outstanding principal of a mortgage may be excluded from taxation, if this mortgage was obtained with the intention of creating or improving the home. Finally, some student loan debts may be excluded from income when canceled.

Gambling winnings

Many taxpayers are surprised to learn that income from legal and illegal gambling is alike subject to full taxation. Legal gambling winnings, such as those from state lotteries and licensed casinos, are reported on Form W-2G, *Certain Gambling Winnings*. Nonprofessional gamblers should report their gross gambling winnings on Form 1040, line 21. A professional gambler should report his or her winnings or losses on Form 1040, Schedule C. In order to qualify as a professional gambler, the taxpayer must be able to prove that wagering represents the better part of his or her professional life. Regardless of the gambler's professional status, losses from gambling can only be deducted from gambling winnings. Therefore, it is impossible for a professional gambler to claim a net loss. Gambling losses are reported as miscellaneous itemized deductions on Schedule A of Form 1040. Gambling losses are not subject to the adjusted gross income floor of 2 percent.

Bartering income

When a taxpayer participates in an economic exchange that does not involve currency, he or she may still be taxed on any items of value that are received. The amount that is subject to taxation is set as the fair market value of the goods at the point of transfer. In most cases, the Internal Revenue Service accepts the fair market value agreed upon by the parties to participate in the exchange. However, in some situations it may be possible to demonstrate that the exchanged item clearly has a different fair market value. Some taxpayers are members of so-called barter clubs, in which people exchange goods and services for other goods and services on a regular basis. Members of barter clubs must include all of the items they receive during the year as income on Form 1099-B, *Proceeds from Broker and Barter Exchange Transactions*. Taxpayers who barter their professional services should report the income received in exchange on Schedule C of Form 1040.

Welfare and other such benefits

State welfare benefits are never subject to taxation, and neither are any payments received from the federal Supplemental Security Income program. Taxpayers will also be exempt from taxation on Medicare, Medicaid, and veterans' benefits. Taxpayers who receive government payments related to disaster relief will be free from taxation as well. However, taxpayers may be required to pay taxes on foster care payments from a state or local government if they care for at least six people over the age of 18. Taxpayers who receive payments because they maintain room in their house for emergency foster care may have to pay taxes as well. Finally, any payments associated with alternative trade adjustment assistance are subject to taxation, and will be reported on Form 1099-G.

Gifts and inheritance income

Gifts are never taxed as income regardless of whether the giver must pay a gift tax. Similarly, any income received as part of an inheritance is free from taxation in most cases. The exceptions to this rule are for taxpayers to receive compensation for acting as the executor of the estate from which he or she inherits. This compensation is treated as other income. The inheritance of a qualified retirement plan or individual retirement account is also subject to taxation when the recipient obtains distributions. If a taxpayer receives property that generates income as part of an inheritance, the income obtained subsequent to the inheritance is subject to taxation.

Self-employment activities

In most cases, the income and expenses related to self-employment activities are reported on Schedule C or Schedule C-EZ, *Profit or Loss from Business*. This is the appropriate place to report any income or expense related to an unincorporated business. Unless the taxpayer is operating a sole proprietorship, the income reported on Schedule C should align with the income reported on Form 1099-MISC or Form 1099-K, *Merchant Card and Third-Party Network Payments*. Any expenses that are considered ordinary and necessary for running the business may be deducted from business income. However, taxpayers are required to keep comprehensive and detailed records to prove the necessity of expenses. The comprehensive guide to self-employment income is IRS Publication 334, *Tax Guide for Small Business*.

Married couples who operate a partnership

Sole proprietors and sole owners of limited liability companies who do not wish to be taxed as corporations will file a Schedule C to report their self-employment information. The only exception is for farmers who are sole proprietors and for whom the appropriate form is Schedule F, *Profit or Loss from Farming*. When a husband and wife are partners in a partnership, the typical protocol is for them to file Form 1065, *United States Return of Partnership Income*. However, one alternative is for each spouse to file a Schedule C return for the partnership and to report their income on separate Schedule K-1s. Spouses who do this are representing themselves as a qualified joint venture, which means that they are the only owners of the business, they both participated in its operation, and they agree to divide all the income, gain, loss, deductions, and credit related to the business.

Schedule C-EZ

Some taxpayers may report their self-employment income on Schedule C-EZ, which is a much less detailed version of Schedule C. However, in order to file this form, the business' expenses must be no more than $5000, and may not require Form 4562, *Depreciation and Amortization*. Also, the business must use the cash method of accounting and have neither a net loss nor passive activity loss carryovers from a previous year. The taxpayer may not use Schedule C-EZ if the business holds any inventory or has any employees during the year. The taxpayer may only own one business, and may not deduct any expenses from business income for business use of his or her home. Unless all of these conditions are met, the taxpayer must report self-employment income on Schedule C.

Schedule C

Basic format
At the top of Schedule C, there is a space for the name of the business proprietor. There is also space where the taxpayer needs to indicate the type of business, such as a wholesale or service business. The taxpayer will also need to indicate the type of goods or services provided, and for whom. This information is indicated in a six-digit business code, which can be obtained in the instructions to Schedule C. The form also includes a space for the taxpayer to indicate whether he or she materially participates in the activities of the business. Material participation is defined as regular, continuous, and substantial engagement with business operations throughout the year. Schedule C also includes a space for indicating the accounting method used by the business. Most businesses that file Schedule C use the cash method, in which income is reported when it is earned and expenses are deducted when paid. Some businesses, however, use the accrual method, in which income and expenses are reported when they are incurred.

Reporting business income
Taxpayers use Schedule C of Form 1040 to indicate business income from self-employment activities. Any business income that is not excludable should be listed on the return. First, the taxpayer will report the gross receipts of the business, which is the total amount of money made from the sale of inventory or provision of services. The amount of returns and allowances is then subtracted from gross receipts, as is the cost of goods sold, yielding the gross profit. The cost of goods sold is essentially the price of all inventory sold during the tax year. Gross profit is then added to any other income, including tax credits and refunds, to produce gross income. The business may need to file Form 1099-MISC to report payments to independent contractors, or Form 1099-K to report merchant transactions on credit and debit cards. Other possible sources of income include the recovery of bad debt or interest earned on accounts receivable.

Reporting of business expenses
A wide variety of business expenses can be listed on Schedule C. For instance, there are spaces for advertising, rent, transportation, and supply expenses. It should be noted that self-employed taxpayers may not deduct their own health insurance premiums or contributions to a qualified retirement plan as a business expense. Instead, these premiums must be deducted as an adjustment to gross income. When the taxpayer uses his own vehicle for business reasons, this expense may be deductible, though it requires comprehensive recordkeeping if the taxpayer wants to deduct the actual expense. Otherwise, he or she may deduct a standard mileage rate. In 2015, the standard mileage

rate was 57.5 cents per mile. It may be necessary for the taxpayer to fill out Part IV of Schedule C in order to deduct the vehicle expense.

Deduction of depreciation expense

Taxpayers who file Schedule C may be able to deduct the expense related to depreciation, which is the decline in value of tangible personal property or real property. It should be noted that land is not subject to depreciation. The amount of depreciation is calculated using the modified accelerated cost recovery system (MACRS), in which assets are divided into various classes that lose their value at different rates. All of this information is listed in tables in IRS Publication 946, *How to Depreciate Property*. Items are considered to begin depreciating once they are placed in service, not when they are purchased. An item cannot depreciate any further after it is taken out of service. In most cases, the adjusted basis (cost of the property) is used as the basis of the property. If the taxpayer converts a piece of personal property into business property, either the adjusted basis or the fair market value at the date of conversion will be used as the basis for depreciation, depending on which is lower.

Bonus depreciation and the Section 179 deduction

The federal government offers a couple of deductions related to depreciation. The deduction for bonus depreciation allows the taxpayer to subtract the entire cost of a new piece of tangible property with a maximum estimated life of 20 years. The bonus depreciation deduction also applies to some building improvements and computers, so long as they are new. This deduction can be applied no matter what the level of taxable income, which means it can even create a net operating loss. Taxpayers will receive the bonus depreciation deduction automatically unless they indicate that they do not wish to receive it. The other deduction related to depreciation is known as the Section 179 deduction. This allows taxpayers to deduct the cost of tangible personal property up to $500,000, so long as the cost of all property placed in service during the tax year does not exceed $2 million. To the extent that property placed in service is greater than $2 million, the $500,000 limit is diminished. Unlike the bonus depreciation deduction, the Section 179 deduction can only be claimed when the business reports a profit and the taxpayer requests it on Form 4562, Part I.

Depreciation related to business vehicles

Vehicles used for business can only depreciate so much. For instance, in 2015, the maximum amount of depreciation for a passenger car in its first year of service was $3,160. These vehicles would also be eligible for $8,000 of bonus depreciation, however. Vehicles are considered to depreciate quite a bit more, at $5,100, in their second year of service. Thereafter, the amount of depreciation decreases markedly. These depreciation limits do not apply to vehicles that cannot be used for personal reasons, such as work vans or heavy trucks. There are also unique depreciation limits for heavy sport-utility vehicles. The complete list of depreciation limits for business vehicles is in IRS Publication 463, *Travel, Entertainment, Gift, and Car Expenses*.

Home office deduction rules

Taxpayers who use part of their home for business purposes may be able to deduct some of their rent/mortgage and utility costs as business expenses. The amount of possible home office deduction can be calculated with Form 8829, *Expenses for Business Use of Your Home*, and then listed on Schedule C. A personal residence does not qualify as a home office unless part of it is used exclusively and frequently as a place for meeting with clients or customers or as the taxpayer's principal place of business. For example, a physical therapist who conducts his or her business at the homes of clients may still be able to deduct the expenses related to his or her home office, if there is a particular room or space that is set aside for administrative work. To claim the home office deduction, the taxpayer will need to separate direct expenses, which are associated only with the home office, and indirect expenses, which are associated with the entire home. Direct expenses are fully deductible, while indirect expenses are prorated according to the percentage of the home that is taken up by the home office.

Casualty and theft losses incurred by a business

Any losses, like theft or casualty that a business suffers and that are not reimbursed are entirely deductible. If the loss was reimbursed in part, the rest of the loss may be deducted. It should be noted that the deduction for casualty and theft losses related to a business is unlimited, unlike the deduction for personal casualty and theft losses. If the taxpayer wants to claim that the casualty or theft loss was related to inventory, the value of the inventory lost can be included in the cost of goods sold expense or reported directly as casualty or theft loss. The business is allowed to claim losses even when they result in a net operating loss. Businesses that claim a net operating loss may carry it back several years and obtain a refund for taxes paid. The protocol for doing so is explained in IRS Publication 536, *Net Operating Losses*.

Schedule F, *Profit or Loss from Farming*

Self-employed farmers and ranchers do not file Schedule C, but instead are required to report their income and expenses on Schedule F, *Profit or Loss from Farming*. This form is similar to Schedule C, but it has specific entries for farm income. The Internal Revenue Service defines a farm as any economic concern involving dairy, poultry, livestock, fish, fruit, or trucks. As with Schedule C, married couples who operate a farm together may apply for status as a qualified joint venture under Schedule F. Any irregular sales of farm property, such as the sale of livestock for breeding, should be reported on Form 4797, *Sales of Business Property*. Taxpayers are required to report income from the sale of crop shares if they materially participate in crop production. Moreover, taxpayers must report any income that comes in the form of government agricultural payments, crop insurance, or crop disaster coverage. By filing Form W-4V, *Voluntary Withholding Request*, farmers may have income taxes withheld on crop insurance and crop disaster payments.

Expenses related to farming

All of the expenses that may be claimed on Schedule C may also be claimed on Schedule F. Furthermore, farmers may claim expenses related to breeding, farm supplies, and soil and water conservation. The extent to which these expenses may be deducted depends on whether the taxpayer uses the cash or accrual method of accounting. For instance, farmers who use the cash method of accounting may not be able to deduct the cost of animal feed and fertilizer if these supplies are purchased in advance. Expenses related to soil and water conservation should be capitalized and added to the cost basis in most cases. Similarly, fees related to animal husbandry should be capitalized and added to the cost basis of the animals produced if the farmer uses the accrual basis of accounting. If the farmer uses the cash basis, on the other hand, breeding fees may be deducted.

Self-employment tax

Self-employed taxpayers pay the self-employment tax, which is calculated on Schedule SE, in order to earn credits for Medicare and Social Security. The basis of the self-employment tax is the net earnings reported on Schedule C or F. Sole proprietors may deduct 7.65 percent of their net earnings before calculating their self-employment tax. Also, self-employed individuals are only subject to the Social Security portion of self-employment tax on the first $117,000 of their income. Medicare tax is applicable to an unlimited amount of earnings. In 2015, the Social Security part of the tax was 12.4 percent and the Medicare part was 2.9 percent. The intention of the self-employment tax is to compile the employee and employer share of the taxes derived from the Federal insurance Contributions Act. The portion of self-employment tax that can be considered the employer's is deductible as an adjustment to gross income.

Hobbies

The Internal Revenue Service classifies activities as hobbies if they are not conducted for profit. A net operating loss is only deductible for activities that cannot be classified as hobbies. If the taxpayer loses money on a hobby, then loss deductions are limited. For instance, the expenses stemming from a hobby may not be deducted in the calculation of the alternative minimum tax. Also, losses related to a hobby may not exceed the income earned by the hobby, and may not be carried over or deducted to the extent they exceed income. Whatever losses are deductible must be classified as miscellaneous itemized deductions on Schedule A, and not on Schedule C or F. These losses are subject to the floor at 2 percent of adjusted gross income.

Profit motive

When evaluating whether an activity is a hobby, the Internal Revenue Service considers whether it is undertaken with a profit motive. There are numerous factors that influence this decision. For instance, the IRS considers the time, effort, and manner in which the activity is performed. The IRS evaluates the skill or knowledge base of the taxpayer with regard to the activity, as well as the possible expectation that assets created or improved during the activity will appreciate in value. The IRS may consider the taxpayer's past income or loss related to the activity, as well as the general financial position of the taxpayer. The IRS may also consider the amount of profit earned from the activity, as well as the joy the taxpayer may receive from performing it. All of these factors are considered when the IRS determines whether the taxpayer is looking to obtain a profit from the activity. If the taxpayer would like to postpone the presumption of a profit motive, he or she must file Form 5213, *Election to Postpone Determination As to Whether the Presumption That an Activity Is Engaged in for Profit*.

Self-employment benefits

In some cases, a self-employed taxpayer may be able to claim deductions based on his or her contributions to a health insurance or retirement plan. These benefits are deductible as adjustments to gross income rather than business expenses. For self-employed taxpayers, the best tax treatment is obtained from retirement plans like solo 401(k)s, savings incentive match plans for employees' individual retirement accounts, and simplified employee pension individual retirement accounts. All of this information is discussed at length in IRS Publication 560, *Retirement Plans for Small Business (SEP, Simple, and Qualified Plans)*. Some taxpayers establish simplified employee pension individual retirement accounts during the extension for filing a tax return, meaning that they are able to reduce their income tax liability after the conclusion of the tax year.

Calculation of property basis

In taxation, a property basis is the extent to which the taxpayer is invested in the property. In many cases, the basis for a piece of property is simply the purchase price. However, when items are improved or when they depreciate, the basis must be adjusted to determine the taxable value of the property. Depletion and amortization are other factors used to calculate adjusted basis. Any claimed basis must be supported by documentation. Taxpayers who fail to provide records may be forced to report zero basis, in which case the entire sale price of the asset will be subject to taxation. The definitive guide to property basis is IRS Publication 551, *Basis of Assets*.

Cost basis

In most cases, property basis is equal to cost, even if the taxpayer does not pay the entire cost of the property at the time of purchase. Cost basis also includes shipping charges, sales taxes, excise taxes, and any related legal or accounting fees. With regard to real property, basis includes any real estate taxes paid by the seller, as well as any settlement costs associated with initiating residence. The property basis of a new property also includes labor, materials, inspection fees, and payments to contractors, architects, and equipment rental services. In cases where several assets are purchased at the same time, or several different buyers are involved, the basis must be allocated according to IRS standards. In a purchase of real property, the taxpayer must separate the basis of land from the basis of buildings, since the land is not subject to depreciation. The separation is based on the fair market value of the building or, if this is unknown, of the land.

Adjusted basis

The extent to which a taxpayer gains or loses money on a property transfer depends on the adjusted basis of the property. Adjusted basis is calculated by taking the original cost of the property and increasing it or decreasing it according to certain factors. For example, improvements and restoration increase basis, while depreciation and easements decrease it. Any capital improvements, like installing better utilities or replacing a roof, increase the basis of the property. However, casualty or theft loss deductions and reimbursements from insurance coverage decrease the basis. The cost of rezoning a property, as well as the legal fees associated with having an assessment reduced or defending and perfecting a title, increases the adjusted basis.

Properties received in exchange for services or similar property

When a taxpayer receives a piece of property in exchange for services, the basis of the property is its fair market value. The rules are slightly different for restricted property, like stocks. If the taxpayer is allowed to sell the property, then the basis is equal to the fair market value. Another option is for the taxpayer to make what is called a Section 83(b) election, such that the fair market value of the stock is included as income when it is received and is treated as the property basis. When property is received in exchange for similar property, known in taxation as an exchange of like-kind property, gains and losses are not recognized or subject to taxation. Like-kind property exchanges, otherwise known as Section 1031 exchanges because of their location in the Internal Revenue Code, can only occur in business.

Properties received as gifts

When property is received as a gift, the basis is determined by its fair market value, adjusted basis according to the giver, and applied gift tax. For the receiver of a gift, the basis is known as carryover basis, because the recipient is assuming the basis previously held by the gift giver. The method used by the taxpayer to calculate basis depends on the relationship between the fair market value of the property and the donor's adjusted basis at the time of the gift. If the fair market value is less than the adjusted basis, then the taxpayer's basis is the same as the donor's adjusted basis when calculating gains. However, when calculating losses the taxpayer should use the fair market value when the property was received. If the fair market value is equal to or greater than the donor's adjusted basis at the time of the gift, then the basis for the gift recipient is the same as the donor's adjusted basis. This basis may be increased if the donor has paid a gift tax.

Inherited property

In most cases, the fair market value on the death date of the decedent is the basis for inherited property. The process of altering the value of the property from the decedent's adjusted basis to the fair market value is known as stepping up, although in some cases the value of the property may be decreased. Occasionally, the executor of an estate may choose to have the property of the deceased assessed at an alternate valuation date. The alternate valuation date is either the date on which the property is distributed or sold or six months after the death of the decedent, whichever comes first. The process of selecting an alternate valuation date is outlined in IRS Publication 559, *Survivors, Executors, and Administrators*.

Property sales, exchanges, and transfers

The Internal Revenue Service distinguishes between property sale, in which property is transferred in return for payment, and exchange, in which property is transferred in return for other property or services. Except in the case of like-kind exchanges, exchanges receive the same tax treatment as sales. There are other transactions that receive the same tax treatment as sales, such as the redemption of stocks and bonds and the full devaluation of nonbusiness bad debts. If the stock or bond loses all of its value during the tax year, it is taxed as if it had been sold on December 31 of that year.

Proceeds from sales

The proceeds of a sale consist of the cash and fair market value of all the property received by the taxpayer. This includes any notes or promises of future payment. Finding the proceeds of the sale enables the calculation of ultimate gain or loss. The gain or loss of the taxpayer is calculated by assessing whether the proceeds of the sale are greater or less than the taxpayer's adjusted basis. In taxation, a gain or loss receives a different tax treatment depending on whether it is defined as capital or ordinary. Ordinary assets are things like real property used in a business, depreciable business property, receivables, inventory, U.S. government notes, and business supplies. Capital assets, on the other hand, include household possessions, personal residences, personal possessions, stocks, bonds, and mutual funds. The protocol for handling the abandonment, repossession, or foreclosure of capital assets is outlined in IRS Publication 4681, *Canceled Debts, Foreclosures, Repossessions, and Abandonments.*

Sales involving related parties

The Internal Revenue Service has established special rules for transactions between related parties, which is to say taxpayers who are members of the same family or business. The point of these rules is to keep taxpayers from unfairly obtaining tax benefits from transfers of capital assets. Any gain from a sale between family members, partners, members of the same corporation, or members of the same charitable or educational organization is treated as ordinary income instead of capital gains, so long as the property in question is subject to depreciation. These same people cannot claim a loss on transactions of capital assets, and neither can the grantor and trustee of a trust, the beneficiary and trustee of a trust, or the beneficiary and executor of an estate.

Holding period for capital assets

With regard to capital assets, the holding period is the length of time that distinguishes short-term from long-term gain or loss. Typically, a holding period of one year or less is considered short term, in which case the capital gains rate is considerably worse for the taxpayer. The maximum rate of taxation for long-term capital gains is 15 percent, whereas short-term capital gains are taxed at the marginal tax rate along with the rest of the taxpayer's ordinary income. Holding period is calculated beginning with the day after the property is first obtained by the taxpayer. With regard to securities, holding period is calculated from the date of the securities purchase rather than settlement date. The holding period for inherited assets is always long term, no matter how long the taxpayer has been in possession of the property. In exchanges of like-kind capital assets, the new property's holding period includes the entire holding period of the property exchanged by the taxpayer.

Reporting sales

In order to report sales on the tax return, the taxpayer needs to indicate whether the gain or loss from the sale is short term or long term, and whether this gain or loss is taxable or nontaxable. The taxpayer will also need to identify whether the gain or loss should receive capital or ordinary taxation. All of this information can be found on information returns received by the taxpayer, including Form 1099-A, *Acquisition or Abandonment of Secure Property*; Form 1099-B, *Proceeds from Broker and Barter Exchange Transactions*; Form 1099-DIV, *Dividends and Distributions*; and Form 1099-S, *Proceeds from Real Estate Transactions*. The taxpayer should record all of the information listed on these information documents exactly as it is given, but if the taxpayer believes some of the information is incorrect, he or she may request a revised information return or report a correction on his or her personal income tax return.

Gains and losses related to capital assets

Form 8949, *Sales and Other Dispositions of Capital Assets*, is the appropriate place for detailing transfers that used to be reported on Schedule D-1, *Continuation Sheet*. All of the information taken from Form 8949 is eventually entered on Form 1040, Schedule D. Form 8949 has two parts, the first of which is for short-term transactions and the latter of which is for long-term transactions. On Form 8949, the taxpayer will have to check one of three boxes to indicate how basis was determined for each transaction of capital assets. If the taxpayer checks Box A, it means that the taxpayer received a Form 1099-B from his or her brokerage firm, and this is the source of the reported basis. If the taxpayer checks Box B, it means that he or she received a Form 1099-B but this form did not indicate his or her basis. This box is checked when the taxpayer acquired the security previous to the tax year in question. Finally, the taxpayer will check Box C if he or she never received a 1099-B form.

Schedule D to compile capital transactions

Taxpayers use Schedule D to compile all of the capital transactions made during the tax year. Schedule D has three parts. All of the short-term transactions described on Form 8949 are carried over onto Part I of Schedule D. Schedule D also includes spaces for short-term capital loss carryover from earlier tax years. At the bottom of Part I, the taxpayer's short-term gains will be compared with his or her short-term losses to find net short-term gain or loss. In Part II, the taxpayer will list all of his or her long-term transactions. There are also spaces here for indicating capital gains distributions from mutual funds and long-term capital loss carryovers from earlier tax years. As with Part I, the long-term gains and losses detailed in Part II are compared to calculate long-term gain or loss. The third part of Schedule D summarizes the totals from the first two parts.

Netting capital gains and losses

There is a precise order for netting capital gains and losses. First, short-term capital losses and gains are compared. When the taxpayer has absorbed a short-term capital loss, this may be used to reduce long-term capital gains. The net amount of capital gains and losses, including those related to both short-term and long-term assets, is subject to a loss limit. It is reported on Form 1040, Schedule D. When a net short-term capital gain exists, it is entered on Form 1040 and taxed at the marginal tax rate like other ordinary income. When there is a net long-term capital gain, it is taxed at 15 percent if the taxpayer's marginal tax rate is higher than 24 percent. If the taxpayer's marginal tax rate is 10 percent or 15 percent, then the tax rate on net long-term capital gains is zero. Net long-term capital gains are taxed at 25 percent, and collectibles gains as well as the non-excluded portion of gain from the sale of qualified small business stock are taxed at 28 percent. The IRS has issued a series of worksheets to assist in making these calculations.

Gains and losses on business assets

Unique tax treatment
When the taxpayer sells business or investment property, special tax rules may apply. For instance, the sale of Section 1244 stock can produce a favorable tax treatment, so long as the taxpayer incurs a loss on the transaction. If the taxpayer incurs a loss on such stock, which is held on certain small businesses, the loss may be classified as an ordinary rather than a capital loss. Similarly, for taxpayers who hold a qualified Section 1202 stock for more than five years and then sell it at a gain, part or all of this gain may be excluded from income. The taxpayer may only exclude an amount equal to 10 times the basis of all the qualified stock related to the corporation in which the taxpayer has ownership, or $10 million less than the eligible gain from stock of that corporation that was excluded by the taxpayer in previous years.

Reporting procedure

The standard form for reporting gains and losses on business assets is 4797. In the first part of this form, the taxpayer will report any sales or exchanges involving business property that has been held for more than one year. The first part of Form 4797 also has a space in which the taxpayer may report gains from involuntary conversions, excluding casualties and deaths. In the second part of Form 4797, the taxpayer can list ordinary gains and losses, which typically involve properties held for less than a year. The third part of the form includes space for reporting gains from the sale of property that is subject to depreciation recapture. The fourth part of Form 4797 includes a space for reporting the Section 179 deduction or situations in which the use of property for business purposes diminishes below 50 percent.

Basis of a home

The main source of information about a homeowner's basis is the price he or she paid for the home, which includes cash and property as well as any mortgage taken on by the purchaser. The basis of a home also includes nondeductible settlement costs, like abstract fees, legal fees, recording fees, title insurance, surveys, and transfer taxes. Any points (1 percent of the amount borrowed) that are paid to obtain a mortgage in the acquisition of the home are fully deductible in the current year, or may be amortized over the full term of the mortgage. If the points are nondeductible, they increase the basis of the home. The basis of a home is also increased by improvements and renovations. Insurance or other reimbursements for casualty losses will decrease the amount of basis, as will depreciation if the home is used for rental or business.

Home sale

Gain or loss

To determine whether a taxpayer has incurred a gain or loss on the sale of a home, he or she needs to know the amount realized on the sale as well as the adjusted basis. By taking the selling price of the home and subtracting all relevant selling expenses, the taxpayer can determine the amount realized on the sale. Selling expenses could include legal fees, brokerage commissions, advertising costs, and loan fees. The adjusted basis is then subtracted from the amount realized on the sale to find the gain or loss. Unlike with business assets or investment properties, it is not possible to recognize a loss on a personal residence, which is viewed the same as any other personal asset. This can be a rude awakening for some taxpayers, who will have considered their home to be an investment; unfortunately, the Internal Revenue Service does not share this opinion.

Home sale exclusion

The taxpayer filing as single may exclude up to $250,000 of gain on the sale of his or her principal residence. Married taxpayers filing jointly may exclude up to $500,000. This exclusion on the sale of a principal residence is only possible if the taxpayer has owned the home for at least two of the last five years, has used the home as a principal residence for at least two of the last five years, and has not excluded gain from the sale of any other home during the past two years. If the taxpayer is using the home as a primary residence but goes on a vacation or sabbatical, this is not considered time spent away from the house. Married couples filing jointly may only get the home sale exclusion if both spouses use the home as a primary residence, one of the spouses qualifies as an owner for two of the past five years, and neither spouse has claimed a home sale exclusion in the past two years. If two unmarried people own the home, each of them may exclude up to $250,000.

Reporting on the tax return

The sale of a principal residence only needs to be reported if part or all of the gain is not excluded, there is a gain that the taxpayer decides not to exclude, or there is a loss resulting in the filing of Form 1099-S, *Proceeds from Real Estate Transactions*. If the taxpayer has realized a gain on the sale of a principal residence and the entire gain can be excluded, the sale does not need to be reported. When there is a taxable gain on the sale of a primary residence, the gain in its entirety must be reported as either short term or long term on Schedule D, *Capital Gains and Losses*, and Form 8949, *Sales and other Dispositions of Capital Assets*. The excluded gain will be indicated as a loss on Schedule D. Taxpayers who sell their homes on installment, meaning that they will receive at least one payment in a subsequent tax year, must file Form 6252, *Installment Sale Income*.

Home abandonments, foreclosures, and repossessions

In most cases, the abandonment, foreclosure, or repossession of a home is treated the same way as a regular sale. Special considerations are required to determine the sale price, however. If the taxpayer is personally liable for repaying the debts of the house, then the selling price must include all of the debt canceled up to the fair market value of the home. In the rare case that the taxpayer is not held personally responsible for the debt, the sale price only includes the amount of debt canceled by repossession or foreclosure. In situations where the canceled debt is greater than the fair market value of the home and the taxpayer is held responsible, the difference between the canceled debt and the fair market value is taxable as ordinary income. An abandoned home will be reported by the bank or the other mortgage holder on Form 1099-A, *Acquisition or Abandonment of Secured Property*.

First-time homebuyer credit

Taxpayers who are purchasing their first home are eligible for the first-time homebuyer credit, though if they sell the home or stop using it as a primary residence part of the credit may be recaptured. If the home was purchased in 2008, and it continues to be owned and used as a principal residence, the credit must be repaid over the next 15 years at a rate depending on the amount of the original credit (for instance, if the entire $7,500 credit was claimed in 2008, the taxpayer must repay $500 every year beginning in 2010). The rate of repayment is calculated with Form 5405, *First-Time Homebuyer Credit and Repayment of Credit*. If the home was purchased in 2008 and the taxpayer sells it or stops using it as a primary residence before the end of the 15-year repayment interval, the balance of credit to be repaid is added to the income tax liability for the year the property is sold or ceases to be used as a primary residence. In the case of involuntary conversion, there is no recapture of the first-time homebuyer credit.

Recapture of the federal mortgage subsidy

Taxpayers who received a federal mortgage subsidy in 1991 or a subsequent year may have this benefit recaptured should they sell the home. A federal mortgage subsidy is either a mortgage credit certificate that reduces the payable income tax in the year of purchase or a reduction of interest rates through financing with a qualified mortgage bond. The amount of recapture is calculated with Form 8828, *Recapture of Federal Mortgage Subsidy*. The federal mortgage subsidy is only recaptured when the home is sold within nine years of the taxpayer receiving the subsidy, and only in situations when the taxpayer's income in the tax year of the sale is larger than the adjusted qualifying income for the size of the taxpayer's family in the year of sale. The federal mortgage subsidy is not subject to recapture if the home is destroyed by a casualty or transferred to a spouse or ex-spouse.

Contributions to traditional IRAs

For the most part, contributions to traditional IRAs are tax deductible. The only exceptions are when a taxpayer has several other retirement plans or an excessive amount of income. To make a tax-deductible contribution to an IRA, the taxpayer must have earned income, which could include self-employment income, wages, tips, combat pay, or alimony payments. Unemployment compensation, pensions, and annuities do not count as earned income for the purposes of IRA contributions. A person may make tax-deductible contributions to an IRA at any age under 70 1/2, though the maximum annual contribution is $5,500. After attaining the age of 70 1/2, a taxpayer may not make a contribution to a traditional IRA. Taxpayers who were at least 50 years old on the last day of 2015 are allowed to contribute an extra $1,000 to their traditional IRA, so long as this contribution does not exceed their earned income for that year. Taxpayers who actively participate in a qualified retirement plan are only allowed the maximum tax-deductible contribution if modified adjusted gross income is not greater than the lowest value in the modified adjusted gross income phase-out range for that taxpayer's filing status.

Contributions to Roth IRAs

Contributions to a Roth IRA are not tax deductible, but earnings from the account do become tax-free if they are held there for at least five years and withdrawn under specific circumstances. Taxpayers are allowed to make contributions to a Roth IRA at any age, so long as they continue to have earned income. However, there are modified adjusted gross income limits for Roth IRA contributions. If the taxpayer is filing as single or as the head of household, he or she may only contribute the maximum amount if modified adjusted gross income is below $117,000. If the taxpayer's modified adjusted gross income is $132,000 or more, no tax-deductible contribution to a Roth IRA is allowed. For married couples filing jointly, a full contribution is allowed if modified adjusted gross income is below $184,000, and no tax-deductible contribution is allowed if modified adjusted gross income is $194,000 or more. The maximum contribution for a Roth IRA is $5,500 for individuals under the age of 50, and $6,500 for individuals age 50 and above.

Contributions to simplified employee pension IRAs (SEP-IRAs)

Taxpayers who have obtained net earnings from self-employment activities are allowed to establish simplified employee pension individual retirement accounts, or SEP-IRAs. The taxpayer is allowed to make payments to these accounts on behalf of him or herself as well as his or her employees, with a maximum contribution of either 25 percent of the participant's compensation or $49,000, whichever is less. One advantage of SEP-IRAs is that they can be established during the extension for the filing of the return, meaning that the taxpayer can establish them and have them take effect retroactively. When a self-employed individual claims a deduction for a contribution to a SEP-IRA, this is done on line 28 of Form 1040; the deduction of contributions made on behalf of employees takes place on Form 1040 Schedule C, *Profit and Loss from Business*.

Savings incentive match plan for employees (SIMPLE) IRAs

Self-employed taxpayers may create a savings incentive match plan for employees (SIMPLE) plan to save for retirement. However, if the self-employed taxpayer operated a business with more than 100 employees, he or she is not eligible for this plan. SIMPLE plans work in much the same way as 401(k) plans: employees make nondeductible contributions before taxes. If an employer establishes SIMPLE plans for his or her employees, he or she is required to make an annual contribution for every eligible employee. Unlike SEP-IRAs, SIMPLE plans must be established during the tax year in which they are claimed; specifically, SIMPLE plans must be established by October 1 of the tax year. However, the employer is allowed to make contributions during the extended due date of his or her tax return.

Tax treatment of contributions to health savings accounts

Taxpayers can avoid being taxed on money that they put aside for medical expenses in a health savings account. However, one prerequisite for contributions to an HSA is health insurance coverage as part of a high-deductible health plan. A high-deductible health plan is one that meets the out-of-pocket limits and annual deductible range that is established by the IRS and modified every year for inflation. Also, the taxpayer must not be receiving health insurance coverage from any other source on the first day of the month in which the contribution takes place. If only the taxpayer is covered, the maximum annual contribution to a health savings account is $3,350. If the entire family of the taxpayer is covered, the maximum annual contribution is $6,650. Taxpayers who have attained the age of 55 by the end of the tax year may contribute another thousand dollars. These contributions are allowed up to the return's due date, and may even be made with tax refunds. They are recorded in Part I of Form 8889.

Educational expense deductions

Most taxpayers will be able to deduct up to $4,000 from their gross income for qualified educational expenses (tuition and fees). The amount of the allowed deduction depends on the modified adjusted gross income of the taxpayer, which in this case does not include the foreign earned income exclusion or the domestic production activities deduction. In order to claim this deduction, the qualified educational expenses must be made on behalf of the taxpayer, the taxpayer's spouse, or a qualified dependent. Any scholarships or educational assistance received from an employer diminishes the amount of qualified tuition and fees. Nondeductible expenses related to education include room and board, transportation, and personal living expenses. The modified adjusted gross income phase-out does not apply to the deduction for tuition and fees, meaning that if the taxpayer's modified adjusted gross income exceeds the limit, the deduction is sharply reduced or forbidden.

In order to claim a deduction for qualified educational expenses, the taxpayer first needs to fill out Form 8917, *Tuition and Fees Deduction*. The resulting deduction is taken away from gross income. The IRS will receive a form from the school (Form 1098-T, *Tuition Statement*) indicating the value of tuition and fees. The taxpayer may only deduct the amount he or she pays, even if he or she is billed for quite a bit more. If the taxpayer made payments in 2015 for classes that began during the first three months of 2016, they may be applied to the 2015 tax year. If the taxpayer receives assistance or a scholarship subsequent to receiving the qualified educational expenses deduction, some of the deduction may need to be reported as income. When this sort of recapture occurs, the taxpayer should calculate the tuition and fees deduction as if the tax-free assistance or refund was given in the same year as the deduction.

Educator expenses deduction

Qualified educators may deduct up to $250 from gross income if they file as single or head of household. Married couples filing jointly who are both educators may deduct up to $500. Expenses qualify for this deduction if they are necessary for the job, like books, technology, athletic equipment, and other school supplies. The Internal Revenue Service considers a person to be an educator if he or she works at least 900 hours per year as a teacher, counselor, instructor, teacher's aide, or principal in grades kindergarten through 12. This deduction is entered on line 23 of Form 1040. If an educator's qualified expenses are greater than $250, the extra amount may be claimed as a miscellaneous itemized deduction (unreimbursed employee business expense).

Student loan interest deduction

Students and former students may deduct up to $2,500 of student loan interest annually. This deduction is taken from gross income, and is only applicable to the principal of the loan. Taxpayers can also claim this deduction if they are obliged to pay interest for a student loan taken out on behalf of their spouse or a dependent. A taxpayer cannot claim this deduction if he or she is married but filing separately or is claimed as a dependent by another taxpayer. Also, if the taxpayer is married filing jointly, he or she cannot receive the full student interest deduction if his or her modified adjusted gross income exceeds $120,000, and, if the taxpayer's modified adjusted gross income is more than $150,000, he or she cannot claim the deduction at all. Taxpayers who file as single or as a head of household may not claim the full deduction if modified adjusted gross income exceeds $60,000, and may not claim any deduction if modified adjusted gross income exceeds $75,000.

Deductions related to self-employment tax

A self-employed taxpayer may deduct one half of his or her employment tax as an adjustment to gross income. This is done so that the self-employed taxpayer will receive the same tax benefits as a typical employer, who would be able to deduct the portion of the employment tax they pay for their employees. This deduction should be claimed on Form 1040, line 27, along with Schedule SE. To claim this deduction, the self-employed taxpayer must have made a profit on the year, and must not be eligible to participate in a health plan, whether administered by his or her employer or a spouse's employer. Similarly, the deduction related to self-employment tax is not legal if the taxpayer is receiving long-term care insurance from an employer or from the spouse's employer.

Moving expense deductions

In situations where a taxpayer is required to move in order to start a new business or take a different job, he or she may be able to deduct moving expenses as an adjustment to gross income. This requires the filing of Form 3903, *Moving Expenses*. The amount of the deduction will then be entered on Form 1040, line 26. However, if the taxpayer has his or her moving costs reimbursed by the employer under an accountable plan, this reimbursement will not be subject to taxation. If the amount of the reimbursement is greater than the moving expenses, or if the moving expenses are reimbursed according to a non-accountable plan, then the taxpayer may only deduct the expenses if he or she incurred the moving expenses within one calendar year of beginning a new job, and if the taxpayer has moved into close proximity to the location of the new job. The only exceptions to this latter condition are if the taxpayer is required to live in the new residence by his or her employer, or if the taxpayer has a reduced cost and duration of commute at the new location.

When a taxpayer must move to start a new business or take a new job, some of the expenses involved in the move may be tax deductible. For instance, all of the costs associated with setting up new utilities and discontinuing old utility services may be deductible. Taxpayers may also be able to deduct the cost of shipping a vehicle or pet. If the taxpayer has to store or insure any of his or her household possessions in the 30 days after moving out of his or her former residence, he or she may be able to deduct this expense. Finally, the taxpayer may be able to deduct the fuel cost of driving to his or her new location. Typically, taxpayers are required to use the standard mileage rate of 19 cents per mile for moving expenses before July 1 and 23.5 cents per mile for moving expenses after June 30. Taxpayers are not allowed to deduct the expenses associated with new driver's licenses, buying a new home, selling an old home, or real estate taxes.

When the taxpayer wants to deduct some of the expenses associated with moving, he or she must calculate the amount of the deduction on Form 3903 and then report it on Form 1040, line 26. If the taxpayer was not reimbursed by his or her employer for these moving expenses, then he or she should claim the deduction for the year in which the expenses were incurred. Taxpayers are allowed to claim the deduction for moving expenses even if they will not have achieved the necessary length of time in the new residence until the next tax year. So long as the taxpayer expects to meet this time threshold in the next year, he or she may claim the deduction. If the taxpayer claims a deduction but unexpectedly fails to achieve the time duration, this deduction may be reported as income on a subsequent tax return or the taxpayer may file Form 1040 X, *Amended US Individual Income Tax Return.*

Alimony

The Internal Revenue Service has established stringent conditions for a payment to be considered alimony. To begin with, the payment must be made in cash, though this may include transfers of electronic funds or payments by check. The payments may not be treated as child support, and must be made under a written separation agreement or a decree of divorce or separate maintenance. The payer and the recipient of alimony payments are not allowed to file a joint tax return, and may not live in the same household at the time of payment. The payment must not be made after the death of the receiving spouse, and the payment must not be labeled as anything other than alimony. In other words, the payment cannot be labeled as part of a property settlement or child support program.

Deduction
A taxpayer who can prove that he or she has made alimony payments may deduct these amounts from gross income. The taxpayer is allowed to deduct an unlimited amount of alimony, no matter how high his or her income, though there are rules to keep taxpayers

from claiming an excessive amount of alimony payments immediately after a divorce or separation settlement (a strategy known as "frontloading" payments). The full amount of the alimony deduction is posted on line 31a of Form 1040. Taxpayers who deduct for alimony payments may not file Form 1040 A or 1040 EZ. Also, the recipient of alimony payments must give his or her Social Security number to the taxpayer responsible for the payments. Otherwise, the recipient spouse may receive a $50 penalty. With regard to individual retirement account and Roth IRA contributions, alimony is considered unearned income; it is not considered as such for the purposes of the earned income tax credit.

Recapture

If the taxpayer has deducted money for alimony payments and these payments are diminished or terminated in their first three years, some of the amount that was deducted in the past must be included in gross income for the third year. (This three-year interval begins in the calendar year in which alimony payments are first made.) If the payments were made according to a temporary support order, this recapture rule does not apply. Alimony payments are often reduced if the recipient spouse no longer needs support, or if there is a change in the separation agreement. Alimony is only recaptured when the payments made in the third year decrease by more than $15,000 from the previous year, or when the payments made in the final two years are significantly less than the payment made in the first year. The Internal Revenue Service has a special formula for determining whether a decrease in alimony payments is significant.

Child support payments

Child support payments may not be taxable for the receiving spouse, and may not be deductible as alimony. In order to qualify as child support, the payment must be explicitly designated as such in a separation agreement or divorce decree. The only case in which a payment not specifically designated as child support may be treated as such is if the payments are reduced upon the child leaving the recipient's home or going to college, or if the payments are terminated at such time. If the child reaches his or her majority and payments then cease, it may be presumed that these payments are child support. However, it is possible for the taxpayer to argue that payments that decrease or terminate upon the child leaving the house are not actually child support.

Deductions and Credits

Standard deduction

The Internal Revenue Service has established standard deduction amounts for all filing statuses. These are set amounts that can be deducted from adjusted gross income in the calculation of taxable income. For taxpayers who file as single or married filing separately, the standard deduction in 2015 was $6,300. Taxpayers who filed as a head of household received a standard deduction of $9,250. Married taxpayers who file jointly and qualifying widows or widowers with a dependent child received a standard deduction of $12,600. Individuals who qualify as blind or who are at least 65 years old received an additional $1,550 on the standard deduction if they filed as head of household, single, or married filing separately, and an additional $1,200 if they filed as married filing jointly or qualifying widow or widower with a dependent child.

Standard deduction for dependents

If the taxpayer could be claimed as a dependent by another taxpayer, he or she in 2015 could claim a standard deduction of either $1,000 or earned income (wages, tips, fees, and self-employment income) plus $350, whichever was greater (so long as the total deduction is no more than $6,300). This standard deduction may also be increased by $1,200 or $1,550 if the dependent is blind or older than 65, depending on the filing status of the taxpayer claiming the dependent. If the taxpayer wants to certify that he or she is blind, or that his or her dependent is blind, medical statements to this effect should be included with the tax records. If the taxpayer is 65 years older and blind, or if his or her dependent is 65 years or older and blind, the taxpayer may claim two additional standard deductions. Also, married couples filing jointly may receive the additional standard deduction for both spouses if they each qualify.

Itemized deductions

Taxpayers usually choose to itemize their deductions or take the standard deduction depending on which will give them the better tax treatment. Married couples filing separately must either both take the standard deduction or both itemize their deductions. If the taxpayer is a nonresident or a dual-status alien, he or she must itemize deductions. The only exception to this rule is if the taxpayer is treated as a resident alien during the tax year; then, he or she may choose the standard deduction. If the taxpayer itemizes the deductions on his or her federal tax return, typically he or she must do so for the state return as well. Itemizing deductions is often a good choice for taxpayers who have contributed a significant amount to charity, who have very high state or local income taxes, who paid a great deal of employee business expenses, who incurred significant property damage not covered by insurance, or who incurred significant medical expenses not covered by insurance.

Deduction of medical and dental expenses

Some taxpayers who have large medical and dental expenses may choose to report them as an itemized deduction. Medical expenses can only be deducted insofar as they exceed 7.5

percent of adjusted gross income. Also, the amount of a deduction for medical expenses is reduced by reimbursements from insurance policies. Taxpayers may also deduct premiums for medical insurance as medical expenses. If the taxpayer is self-employed and is claiming an annual profit, he or she may deduct any premiums paid for him or herself, his or her spouse, and his or her children under the age of 27. This deduction for self-employed individuals is registered as an adjustment to income, and does not need to be itemized. However, it should be noted that deductions related to medical insurance premiums are also subject to the floor at 7.5 percent of adjusted gross income.

Taxpayers are allowed to deduct medical expenses incurred on behalf of themselves, their spouses, and their children under the age of 27, even if these children cannot be claimed as dependents. In order to claim the deduction for the medical expenses of a spouse or dependent, the individual for whom the services were provided must have been the spouse or dependent at the time the services were provided. It is not necessary; however, that the relationship still be in place at the time the deduction is claimed. In other words, a taxpayer may claim a deduction for his or her spouse's medical expenses even if the taxpayer has gotten divorced in the interval between the provision of services and the filing of the tax return. Taxpayers are allowed to deduct medical expenses related to children under the age of 27 even if those children cannot be claimed as dependents, so long as the child would qualify as a dependent if he or she had not filed a joint return, had not had a gross income exceeding $4,000 in 2015, or had not been claimed as a dependent by another taxpayer.

Special circumstances in which medical costs may be deducted
If the taxpayer has incurred medical or dental expenses for a child he or she has legally adopted, these expenses may be deducted. Similarly, payments made to an adoption agency for medical expenses for a child subsequently adopted may be deducted. Medical expenses for a child of divorced parents may be deducted by the paying parent, even if he or she cannot claim the child as a dependent. Taxpayers can also deduct medical expenses they pay for anyone for whom they provide more than half of support under a multiple support agreement. If the taxpayer incurs medical expenses for a spouse or dependent who subsequently dies, these expenses should be listed on the Form 1040 for the year in which they are paid. Finally, a taxpayer who dies during the tax year may have his or her medical expenses incurred before death deducted on his or her final tax return, though these medical expenses are still subject to the floor at 7.5 percent of adjusted gross income.

Qualified medical expenses
Medical expenses qualify for deduction if they are related to treatment for the alleviation or prevention of a physical or mental defect or illness. Medical expenses related to health promotion or maintenance may not be deductible. Diagnostic services and laboratory tests are typically deductible, as are basic fees to doctors and other medical practitioners. Premiums for health insurance, including Medicare and COBRA coverage, are deductible. Any expenses related to qualified long-term care in a nursing home or hospital is deductible, as are any payments for medication, medical equipment, and health supplies. There is a limit to the deduction that may be taken for long-term care insurance: individuals age 40 or younger may only deduct $340, but the deductible limit increases with age until it maxes out at $4,240 for taxpayers over the age of 70. The cost of travel for medical reasons may be deducted at the standard rate of 19 cents per mile for travel before July 1 and 23.5 cents per mile for travel after June 30.

Non-deductible medical expenses

Taxpayers may not claim a deduction for medical expenses incurred for cosmetic or strictly health-promoting reasons. For example, taxpayers may not claim a deduction for plastic surgery unless it is necessary to correct a serious medical condition. Basic toiletries and personal hygiene products are not deductible, and neither are over-the-counter medications, nutritional supplements, and vitamins. Expenses related to cremation, funeral, or burial are not deductible. Any medical expenses that are reimbursed from health plans are not deductible. Home improvements are only deductible if they are designed to mitigate a health problem; for instance, installing a handrail for a disabled person would be a deductible expense. Home improvements are only fully deductible, though, to the extent that they do not raise the fair market value of the home.

Protocol for determining which taxes may be deducted

There are three conditions that must be met in order for a tax to be deductible. The first condition is that the tax must be imposed on the taxpayer specifically. The tax must be one that is subject to deduction, and it must be paid during the tax year in question. The IRS considers that a tax has been paid on the date on which it is mailed, so long as the taxpayer has enough money to cover the expense. If the taxpayer paid the tax through an electronic transfer or over the phone, then the payment is reported as having been made on the date on which it appears on the account statement. The following taxes are deductible: taxes on business expenses; state and local income taxes; state and local sales taxes; occupational taxes; state and local real estate taxes; foreign real estate taxes; and state and local personal property taxes.

Taxes that are not deductible

Any fees or charges related to personal pursuits, like auto repair or utilities, are typically not tax deductible. Federal income taxes are not tax deductible, and neither are any employee contributions to a private or voluntary disability fund. The following miscellaneous taxes are not deductible: per capita tax, estate tax, inheritance tax, gift tax, transfer tax, stamp tax, and federal excise tax not related to property that produces income. Any customs duties paid on property that produces income are not tax deductible. Taxpayers are not allowed to deduct any fees for municipal services or taxes for local benefits. If the taxpayer's rent is increased because of higher local real estate taxes, the taxpayer may not deduct this cost. Finally, taxpayers are not allowed to deduct fees related to joining a homeowners' association.

Deduction of state and local income and sales taxes

Any state or local income taxes that are paid through withholding, direct payment to the state, or estimated taxes may be deducted. Married couples who file jointly may deduct the full amount of state and local income taxes paid by both spouses. Married couples who file separately are only allowed to deduct the state and local income taxes paid by each individually. In most cases, taxpayers can also deduct or claim a tax credit for foreign income taxes and state and local sales taxes. The amount of the deduction related to sales taxes can be calculated by using the optional sales tax table provided by the IRS in Schedule A or by adding up receipts. Obviously, the latter method requires excellent recordkeeping. If the taxpayer lived in multiple states during the year, sales tax must be apportioned according to the percentage of the tax in the state and the number of days lived there.

Deduction of real estate taxes

For the most part, a taxpayer may claim an itemized deduction for state, local, or foreign real estate taxes, so long as the property is not used for business or profit (i.e., it is not a rental property). The taxpayer may claim this deduction on any number of properties, but each of these deductions must be itemized. There is no standard deduction for real estate taxes. If the taxpayer buys or sells a property in the middle of the tax year, the amount of real estate taxes is apportioned according to the number of days during the year in which the taxpayer owned the property. A taxpayer who sells a property is not considered to own it on the date of sale. If the taxpayer receives a refund of real estate taxes in the same year, the deduction is reduced accordingly.

Deduction of home mortgage interest

In most cases, taxpayers can deduct any interest paid on debt related to purchasing, constructing, or improving a main or secondary home. However, taxpayers may only consider up to $1 million of acquisition debt in the calculation of this deduction. Taxpayers may also deduct interest related to home equity debt, though this debt may not exceed the fair market value of the home or $100,000, whichever is less. Also, home equity debt interest cannot be deducted for the purposes of the alternative minimum tax unless the debt was incurred to improve the home. In order to qualify for the interest deduction, the taxpayer must itemize and must have his or her mortgage or loan secured by a home. The amount of interest paid is reported on Form 1098, *Mortgage Interest Statement*.

Deduction of mortgage insurance premiums

Taxpayers are allowed to deduct private mortgage insurance premiums like any other home mortgage insurance. However, it is necessary that the insurance contract has been issued in 2007 or later. The extent to which these premiums are deductible is based on the adjusted gross income of the taxpayer. Adjusted gross income of $100,000 or less allows the full amount to be deducted, but if the adjusted gross income is greater than $109,000, no deduction may be claimed. In most cases, mortgage insurance is purchased from the Rural Housing Service, the Federal Housing Administration, the Department of Veterans Affairs, or a private company. It is necessary when the taxpayer cannot afford to pay 20 percent of the purchase price of the home.

Deduction related to investment interest

If the taxpayer incurs debt as part of the purchase of investment property, he or she may be able to deduct the interest expense related to this debt. A property is considered an investment if it produces income. If the taxpayer uses the cash basis of accounting, then he or she may deduct this interest when it was paid. Taxpayers may not deduct the expense related to interest that is paid to produce tax-exempt income, or interest that must be capitalized under the uniform capitalization rules. Taxpayers are not allowed to deduct home mortgage interest, or interest on a loan used to purchase an annuity or life insurance contract. Investment interest is reported on Schedule A. The amount of the deduction related to investment interest may not exceed net in investment income for the year.

Organizations to which taxpayer may make deductible donations

Donations to qualified organizations may be deductible. The Internal Revenue Service declares that any organization established for religious, educational, scientific, charitable, or humanitarian reasons may receive tax-deductible donations. Donations to veterans' organizations in the United States are tax deductible, as are donations to American fraternal societies and associations operating under a lodge system. Taxpayers may deduct donations to nonprofit cemetery companies or corporations, so long as these donations are put to a general use. Finally, any donations to a state or subdivision of the United States may be tax deductible if they are directed toward public service. IRS Publication 78, *Cumulative List of Organizations*, provides a comprehensive summary of the institutions eligible for tax-deductible donations.

If the taxpayer contributes to a qualified organization but also receives a benefit from that organization (for instance, the taxpayer purchases a ticket to a charity ball), the taxpayer may only deduct the difference between the amount contributed and the value of the benefit. The taxpayer is required to assess the fair market value of the benefit. There are some specific rules related to this type of transaction. For instance, if a taxpayer contributes to a college or university and receives the option to purchase tickets to an athletic event, the taxpayer may only deduct 80 percent of the contribution. If the taxpayer purchases a ticket to a charity ball, the taxpayer may only deduct the difference between the donation and a reasonable value for the ticket. This is true even when the ticket declares itself to be fully tax deductible. Although annual fees to religious institutions are fully deductible, other dues that enable a person to gain admission to meetings or ceremonies are only partially deductible.

Property donations
When a taxpayer donates property to a qualified organization, the fair market value of the property is deductible. In cases where the fair market value is unknown, the taxpayer may have the property appraised and deduct the cost of the appraisal as a miscellaneous itemized deduction. If the donated property is defined as capital gains property, the fair market value of the property is fully deductible. If it is ordinary income property, the taxpayer may only deduct the fair market value less the amount of ordinary income or short-term capital gain the taxpayer would realize on the sale of the property. In other words, a taxpayer cannot make a profit by donating property that has appreciated in value since its purchase. If the property has decreased in value in the interval between its purchase and its donation, the taxpayer may only deduct the fair market value of the property at the time of the donation.

Recordkeeping for cash contributions
A taxpayer may only claim a deduction on a cash contribution to a qualified organization if he or she has a bank record, a receipt, a letter from the organization, or a payroll deduction indicating the date and the amount of the contribution. If the contribution was for $250 or more, the taxpayer must provide a payroll deduction record or a written form from the qualified organization. These requirements hold for each donation of $250 or more, even when made to the same organization. The written form from the qualified organization must declare the amount of the cash contribution and the date. Any out-of-pocket expenses incurred by the taxpayer on behalf of a qualified organization are considered like cash contributions, and must likewise be accompanied by a written form from the qualified organization if the taxpayer is to receive a deduction.

Required recordkeeping for non-cash contributions

When the taxpayer donates property to a qualified organization, he or she must obtain certain records. If property is worth less than $250, the taxpayer needs to provide a receipt from the organization. This receipt should include a decent description of the property, the name of the qualified organization, and the date and location of the contribution. The taxpayer should maintain records of the property donations he or she makes to qualified organizations, even if these donations are valued at less than $250. If the taxpayer donates property that is worth at least $250 but no more than $500, he or she must obtain a written acknowledgment from the charitable organization indicating the characteristics, date, and location of the donation. If the taxpayer makes a donation of property with a value of more than $500 but less than $5,000, the taxpayer will also need to submit forms indicating how and when he or she acquired the property, as well as the cost or basis of the property. If a taxpayer donates property worth more than $5,000, he or she will need to submit a qualified written appraisal from a certified appraiser along with all of the information required for smaller donations.

Timing of deductions
Contributions to qualified charitable organizations may only be deducted in the year of the donation. This is true even when the donation is made with borrowed funds that are repaid in a different tax year. With regard to mailed donation checks, the date of the donation is considered to be the date on which the check is mailed. As for donations that are made with credit cards, the donation is considered to have occurred on the date on which the card is charged. If the taxpayer calls his or her financial institution and requests that they make a payment to a charitable organization, the donation is dated as having occurred when the financial institution makes payment, and not when the taxpayer makes the request. If the taxpayer sells the qualified organization an option to purchase property at a reduced price in the future, the donation is not said to occur until the organization exercises this option.

Limits on deductions
If the taxpayer's total donations to qualified organizations are equal to 20 percent or less of his or her adjusted gross income, then these donations are fully deductible. However, some capital gain property may not be eligible for deduction if it represents between 20 percent and 50 percent of the taxpayer's adjusted gross income. Most public charities are defined as 50 percent limit organizations, meaning that a taxpayer's donations are deductible up to 50 percent of adjusted gross income. If the taxpayer makes a charitable contribution that exceeds the adjusted gross income limit, the excess may be carried forward until it is fully deducted, so long as this can be done within five years. The Internal Revenue Service does not allow carryback for charitable contributions that exceed the limits.

Nondeductible contributions to charitable organizations

Taxpayers are not allowed to deduct any contributions made directly to needy individuals. In other words, a taxpayer may not deduct contributions made to panhandlers, but may deduct contributions made to organizations that provide meals for the homeless. Taxpayers may not deduct contributions from which the taxpayer derived a benefit, such as contributions to state lotteries or nonprofit day care centers. Taxpayers may not deduct the value of any time or material expense related to volunteer work. The donation of blood, plasma, or organs is not tax deductible. Also, any contributions to qualified organizations that could be considered personal expenses are not deductible. For instance, if a taxpayer makes a contribution to a nonprofit agency as part of adopting a child, this expense is not deductible.

Loss

Nonbusiness casualty and theft losses

Taxpayers may claim as an itemized deduction any casualty or theft losses for which they are not reimbursed, by insurance or otherwise. However, before these amounts are deducted from income, each individual loss is diminished by $100, and the total amount of casualty and theft loss is decreased by 10 percent of adjusted gross income. Taxpayers who suffer a disaster loss may claim the deduction on the return for the current or prior year. If the taxpayer claims a deduction for casualty or theft loss, he or she must accordingly decrease the basis of the property in question. However, if the taxpayer spends money to restore the value of a property after a casualty or theft, this increases the property basis. If the taxpayer receives a reimbursement that is greater than the adjusted basis of the property, he or she may realize a gain subsequent to casualty or theft loss. If it would result in a more favorable tax treatment, the taxpayer is allowed to put off this gain until a future tax year.

Casualties and related but nondeductible losses

In most cases, losses are deductible if they result from a sudden, unexpected, or unusual event, otherwise known as a casualty. Some of the most common casualty events are fires, floods, earthquakes, car accidents, tornadoes, and hurricanes. If the casualty is the result of the taxpayer's willful act or negligence, however, damage or destruction to property is not deductible. Similarly, taxpayers are not allowed to deduct money related to the gradual or slow deterioration of property, such as crops lost to drought or the weakening of building foundations by normal weather conditions. In order to demonstrate that a deductible casualty loss has occurred, the taxpayer should have documentation about the casualty, including its characteristics and date. The taxpayer should also be able to prove that the loss was a direct result of the casualty, and that the taxpayer was indeed the owner of the property in question. The taxpayer should also be able to demonstrate whether there is a competing claim for reimbursement or a reasonable expectation of recovery.

Loss due to theft

According to the Internal Revenue Service, theft is the act of taking money or property away from its rightful owner. Some of the most common varieties of theft are blackmail, extortion, burglary, robbery, fraud, embezzlement, and kidnapping for ransom. Property loss or disappearance is not the same thing as theft, and does not receive the same favorable tax treatment if it does not qualify as a casualty. In most cases, the decline in the value of investments does not qualify as a casualty loss. However, if the taxpayer loses money in a Ponzi (pyramid) investment scheme, this loss may be defined as theft. Moreover, in some situations the taxpayer may be able to deduct losses of this type even if claims against the thief are ongoing. In order to prove that property was stolen, a taxpayer will need to have records indicating when he or she discovered it was missing, that he or she was indeed the owner of the property, and whether he or she has made a reimbursement claim with a reasonable expectation of recovery.

Loss on deposits

When a taxpayer makes a deposit in a financial institution and the deposit is lost due to the institution's bankruptcy or insolvency, the taxpayer may deduct this loss in a few different ways. To begin with, the taxpayer may deduct the loss as a nonbusiness bad debt, though this cannot be done until the tax year in which the precise value of the loss can be calculated. Nonbusiness bad debts are reported on Form 8949, *Sales and Other Dispositions of Capital Assets*, and Schedule D of Form 1040. Taxpayers may also deduct a loss on deposits as an ordinary loss, which is reported as a miscellaneous itemized deduction on Schedule A. The taxpayer may claim no more than $20,000 of losses of this type, less any proceeds from state insurance. Deposit losses that are claimed as ordinary losses are subject to the normal limit on miscellaneous itemized deductions, at 2 percent of adjusted gross income. Finally, a taxpayer may deduct deposit loss as a casualty, with the usual limits. Casualty losses are reported on Form 4684, *Casualties and Thefts*, and Schedule A of Form 1040.

Calculating casualty or theft loss
The calculation of casualty or theft loss depends on the adjusted basis of the property before the event. The taxpayer must then determine the amount of decline in the fair market value of the property. Of course, in the case of stolen property, the fair market value becomes zero. In many cases, the taxpayer will need to obtain an appraisal before determining the change in fair market value. The cost of this appraisal may not be considered part of the casualty loss. The loss deductible due to casualty or theft loss is the adjusted basis or the decrease in fair market value, whichever is less. Also, however, the taxpayer must reduce the smaller value by any reimbursement. If the taxpayer receives a reimbursement that is greater than the adjusted basis of the property, he or she may wait to be taxed on this gain.

Adjustments to the amount of casualty loss made for reimbursements
When calculating the amount of casualty loss, taxpayers must subtract any reimbursements, whether from insurance, an emergency disaster fund, or other sources. Taxpayers are not required to count any money received from friends and relatives as a reimbursement. Also, any reimbursements specifically allocated for living expenses do not need to be deducted from the amount of casualty loss. Similarly, any disaster relief payments for medical supplies or food are not considered as reimbursement. There are special tax rules related to reimbursements that occur after the claiming of a deduction. For instance, if the taxpayer recovers stolen property after claiming a loss due to theft, the taxpayer should recalculate the loss by comparing the decrease in fair market value from the date of theft to the recovery date with the property's adjusted basis, and then taking the smaller of the two values. If the taxpayer expected to receive a greater reimbursement then he or she ended up receiving, the difference may be counted as a loss on his or her tax return.

Expenses that cannot be deducted as miscellaneous itemized deductions

Bank account fees related to personal accounts cannot be deducted as miscellaneous itemized deductions; these are considered to be nondeductible personal expenses. Any membership fees associated with business or social clubs are not deductible, unless membership in a health club has been prescribed by a doctor. Any donations to political campaigns are not deductible, nor are any expenses related to running for public office oneself. Expenses incurred while commuting to and from work are not deductible. Expenses related to adopting a child are not deductible as a miscellaneous itemized deduction, though they may be used to obtain a tax credit. The payment of fines and penalties may not be deducted, and neither can any legal fees associated with personal defense. Expenses associated with professional accreditation cannot be deducted. Finally, any costs associated with personal living, like home furnishings and groceries, may not be deducted.

Work expenses

Employee business expenses

Many of the costs an employee incurs during the performance of his or her job are deductible. Deductible employee business expenses are limited to those that exceed 2 percent of adjusted gross income. To report business expenses, employees must file Form 2106, *Employee Business Expenses*, or Form 2106 EZ, *Unreimbursed Employee Business Expenses*, and then enter the net amount on Form 1040, Schedule A. Employee business expenses are only deductible when they are necessary to the performance of the job, and could be assumed by a reasonable person to be a normal part of the job. Personal expenses and capital expenditures (that is, expenses that add to the basis of property) are not deductible. Similarly, employees may not deduct expenses related to commuting, professional accreditation, or fines and penalties related to business travel.

Travel

When an employee must travel away from his or her tax home for a period longer than a normal day of work, such that he or she will sleep away from home, this expense is deductible. For employees, a tax home is defined as the regular place of business, irrespective of the location of the personal residence. In some situations, an employee may use his or her residence as a tax home, provided he or she has no regular place of business, performs some of his or her work at home, lives in the home, and has his or her living expenses at home duplicated when he or she is away. If the taxpayer does not meet all of these conditions, then he or she is considered a transient for tax purposes, and his or her tax home is defined as wherever he or she performs work for compensation. If the taxpayer has a different tax home from his or her family, the cost of travel to and from the family home is not deductible. Moreover, a taxpayer may not deduct any costs associated with room and board while at his or her tax home.

Expenses related to operating and maintaining a car while away from home on business are deductible, even if the car in question is a rental. Taxpayers are allowed to collect receipts and deduct the actual expense of operating the car, or they may deduct the standard mileage rate. Taxpayers may also deduct the costs of traveling by train, airplane, bus, or car to and from the business destination. However, taxpayers who receive a discounted or free ticket because of a frequent traveler program may not deduct any cost for travel. Taxpayers are also allowed to deduct the cost of lodging and meals if the trip is long enough to require these. Taxpayers may deduct the cost of any business calls made while away from the tax home, and may also deduct the costs of dry cleaning and laundry while away from the tax home on business.

Business gifts

Taxpayers are allowed to deduct the expense of gifts purchased in the normal course of their job. The limit on deductions for business gifts is $25 per year per recipient, though this does not include incidental costs related to gift giving, like postage, insurance, and giftwrapping. These incidental costs may be deducted separately. The cost of entertainment related to business may only be deducted 50 percent. In some cases, it may be difficult to tell the difference between gifts and entertainment. When in doubt, the tax preparer should usually classify the expense as entertainment. When a taxpayer purchases tickets to an event for a client or coworker, this expense is considered entertainment if the taxpayer attends the event as well, and as a gift if the taxpayer does not.

Local transportation expense for business

Taxpayers may be able to deduct some of the costs of transportation even if they are not far away from their tax home. For instance, taxpayers may be able to deduct the expense of traveling to visit suppliers, customers, or vendors. Taxpayers may be able to deduct the cost of traveling from the workplace to a business meeting, though the expense of commuting from home to work is not deductible. The only exception to the rule involving commutes is when the taxpayer incurs an extra expense for hauling equipment. If the taxpayer has more than one job, he or she may be able to deduct the cost of traveling from one job to the other. If the taxpayer has used his or her personal car for business travel, he or she may deduct the actual expense, or may use the standard mileage rate established by the IRS: in 2015, this rate was 57.5 cents per mile. Taxpayers are also allowed to deduct the cost of parking and tolls while out on business.

Work-related educational expenses

Taxpayers may be able to deduct some of the expenses of professional advancement education if they are not reimbursed by their employer. So long as the education is required by the employer or by law or it maintains the employee's skills for his or her current job, professional educational expenses may be listed as a miscellaneous itemized deduction. Taxpayers may not deduct the cost of education that is necessary to meet the minimum requirements for the taxpayer's current job. Similarly, the taxpayer may not deduct the cost of any education that will help him or her qualify for a new job. In order to claim work-related educational expenses, then, the taxpayer must be employed while the education is received. In some cases, a taxpayer on a temporary leave may deduct educational expenses. The types of educational expenses that are typically deductible are books, tuition, fees, school supplies, and transportation costs. Students are allowed to deduct transportation costs according to the standard mileage rate.

Maintaining records for business deductions

In order to deduct expenses incurred during the normal course of business, an employee must maintain good records. The expense records must include the type of expense, the date, and any other necessary information. The extra information required depends on the nature of the expense. For instance, if a taxpayer has incurred business travel expenses, he or she needs to have a document indicating the destination, the dates of departure and arrival, the itemized costs associated with the trip, and the business purpose of the trip. Business entertainment expenses must be itemized as well, and the taxpayer's documentation must include the name and address of the venue. Moreover, entertainment and gift expenses must be accompanied by a description of the customer, vendor, or supplier who is the recipient. Business transportation expenses must be itemized, dated, and described.

Reimbursement of employees for business-related expenses under accountable and non-accountable plans

When an employer establishes a specific plan for reimbursing employees for business-related expenses, this is known as an accountable plan. In a typical accountable plan, the employer reimburses the employee for out-of-pocket expenses or establishes a method for paying expenses directly (for instance, with a company credit card). The employer will then deduct the business expense. An employer does not have to report reimbursement to employees on W-2 forms, because this expense is not considered compensation. The reimbursement program only qualifies as an accountable plan if it has a clear business connection, if it requires the employee to accurately describe expenses to the employer within 60 days, and if employees are required to return excess reimbursement within 120 days. If the plan does not meet all of these criteria, it is considered non-accountable, and reimbursements must be reported on a Form W-2 as compensation.

Per diems
The IRS has established various per diem rates, which obviate the need for the employee to record precise amounts for business expenses. This does not mean, however, that the employee is not required to maintain sufficient records related to business expenses. The greatest per diem rate is called the regular federal rate: this is the rate paid by the United States government to its employees for room and board while traveling on government business. The IRS also allows the standard meal allowance, which is a prorated amount appropriate for travel of less than one full day, for localities in the continental United States. Finally, taxpayers may use what is called the high-low method, wherein employers may use one of two rates for employee per diems, depending on whether the employee is traveling in a high-cost area. The IRS lists high-cost areas in Publication 1542.

Earned income credit

The earned income credit reduces the tax liability for working taxpayers who make less than a certain amount. If the earned income credit is greater than the tax owed during the year, the amount of the excess is refundable. In general, the value of an earned income credit is based on income and number of qualifying children. This credit may be claimed on Form 1040, Form 1040 A, or Form 1040 EZ. In 2015, the maximum earned income credit for a taxpayer without qualifying children was $503. If the taxpayer had one qualifying child, the maximum earned income credit was $3,359; if the taxpayer had two qualifying children, the maximum earned income credit was $5,548; and if the taxpayer had three or more qualifying children, the maximum earned income credit was $6,242. Taxpayers are no longer able to receive the earned income credit in advance if they have a qualifying child.

Income qualifications
In order to receive the earned income credit, the taxpayer must make less than the limit established for his or her filing status. There is a phase-out range, within which the taxpayer may be eligible for a reduced earned income credit. The taxpayer must also have earned some of his or her income, meaning that it must arrive as net earnings from self-employment, wages, salary, or tips. Taxpayers may not treat dividends, pensions, annuities, Social Security benefits, child support, welfare, unemployment compensation, workers' compensation, and veterans' benefits as earned income. However, members of the military who receive combat pay that is not subject to taxation may report it as earned income. If the taxpayer claims the foreign earned income exclusion on Form 2555, he or she may not claim the earned income credit. Taxpayers are also not allowed to claim the earned income credit if their investment income (which includes capital gains distributions, ordinary and qualified dividends, royalties, rental income, and all forms of interest) exceeds a certain amount.

Number of qualifying children
A taxpayer is able to claim a larger earned income credit if he or she has qualifying children. To qualify, the child must be the biological descendent, stepchild, adopted child, foster child, sibling, step sibling, half sibling, or any descendent of one of these relations of the taxpayer. The child must also be 18 years or under at the end of the year, and must be younger than the taxpayer. If the child is enrolled as a full-time student for at least five months during the

year, he or she may be up to the age of 24. To qualify for the purposes of the earned income credit, a child must also live with the taxpayer for at least half the year. Finally, the child cannot be claimed for the purposes of the earned income credit if he or she has filed a joint return, unless this return was filed for the sole purpose of receiving a tax refund. Taxpayers are not allowed to divide the tax benefits related to qualifying children.

Taxpayers without a qualifying child
If the taxpayer does not have a qualifying child, he or she may still obtain the earned income credit so long as he or she is between the ages of 25 and 65 on December 31 of the tax year. Married couples who file jointly only need to have one individual within this age range. Also, a taxpayer without a qualifying child may not claim the earned income credit if he or she is a qualifying child or a dependent of another person. Also, in order to claim the earned income credit a taxpayer must have lived in the United States for at least half the year. A taxpayer cannot claim the earned income credit if he or she is married filing separately. Also, taxpayers cannot claim the earned income credit if they claim the foreign earned income exclusion or make a deduction for foreign housing. Finally, if the taxpayer actually has a qualifying child, he or she cannot claim the earned income credit as if he or she did not have the qualifying child.

Calculation
The precise value of the earned income credit is determined on a table produced by the IRS. The factors involved in the calculation of the credit are the filing status of the taxpayer, his or her number of qualifying children, and his or her income. As an example, in 2015 taxpayers who filed as single, a qualifying widow(er), or a head of household could claim the earned income limit if they had one child and made less than $39,131. It is important to note that deferred compensation, scholarships, and fellowships are not considered earned income. The earned income credit is calculated on one of two worksheets. Taxpayers will use EIC Worksheet A if they were not self-employed, a member of the clergy, a statutory employee, or a church employee with self-employment income. Taxpayers will use EIC Worksheet B if they were self-employed, a member of the clergy, a statutory employee, or a church employee with self-employment income.

Child and dependent care credit

The child and dependent care credit is claimed on Form 2441, *Child and Dependent Care Expenses*, which accompanies the 1040 form. The size of a child and dependent care credit depends on adjusted gross income and number of qualifying children or dependents, but, unlike the earned income credit, it does not depend on the taxpayer's filing status. The child and dependent care credit is only for taxpayers who go to school or work full time. If the taxpayer has one qualifying child or dependent, he or she may claim up to $3,000 of work-related care expenses; if the taxpayer has more than one qualifying child or dependent, he or she may claim up to $6,000. The amount of the credit is between 20 percent and 35 percent of qualifying expenses, meaning that the maximum child and dependent care credit for taxpayers with one qualifying child or dependent was $1,050 in 2015.

Work-related expenses
The typical expenses that are eligible for the child and dependent care credit are those that enable the taxpayer to work, look for work, or go to school, or which cover the cost of child or dependent care. For example, a taxpayer may be able to claim a credit for money paid to a babysitter, day care center, or day camp. Taxpayers are not allowed to claim the credit for

the cost of overnight camp. Taxpayers may be able to claim credit for the expense of transporting the child to and from the place of care. Taxpayers may be able to claim the credit for prekindergarten programs (i.e., nursery school or preschool). If the child is in kindergarten or a higher grade, the taxpayer may be able to claim the credit for expenses related to before-school or afterschool care.

Child tax credit

Taxpayers with a qualifying child under the age of 17 may be eligible for a tax credit. For 2012 and beyond, the maximum amount of the child tax credit was $1,000. Taxpayers may receive a separate credit for each child they can claim. The child tax credit is nonrefundable, and can only be used to reduce a tax liability. Claiming the child tax credit does not preclude the taxpayer from also claiming the child and dependent care credit. However, taxpayers who make over a certain amount of money may receive only a partial child tax credit, or may not receive any child tax credit. To qualify for this credit, the child must be the taxpayer's direct descendent, stepchild, foster child, sibling, step sibling, or some descendent of one of these relations. Also, in order to qualify, a child must be 16 or younger at the end of the year, and must be younger than the taxpayer who is claiming him or her. A child does not qualify if he or she did not live with the taxpayer for at least half the year, and if he or she provided at least half of his or her own support during the tax year. Finally, a qualifying child must be a United States citizen, United States resident alien, or United States national.

Value
In general, the child tax credit is worth $1,000 for each qualifying child. However, the amount of child tax credit is limited to the taxpayer's liability. Also, if the taxpayer's modified adjusted gross income exceeds a threshold amount for his or her filing status, the amount of child tax credit is reduced by $50 for each excess $1,000 of modified adjusted gross income. Remember that modified adjusted gross income is simply adjusted gross income plus the foreign earned income exclusion. For 2012 and beyond, the modified adjusted gross income threshold for taxpayers who filed as single, head of household, or qualifying widow(er) was $75,000. For married taxpayers who filed jointly, the threshold for modified adjusted gross income was $110,000. For married taxpayers who filed separately, the modified adjusted gross income threshold was $55,000.

Additional child tax credit
If the tax liability of a taxpayer is less than the amount of the regular child tax credit to which he or she is entitled, the taxpayer may be able to claim the additional child tax credit. However, the additional child tax credit cannot be greater than the maximum child tax credit (i.e., $1,000 in most cases). Form 8812, *Additional Child Tax Credit*, indicates that the value of the tax credit is either the amount of child tax credit left over after the alternative minimum tax or regular taxes are set to zero, or 15 percent of earned income over $3,000, whichever is smaller. If the taxpayer has three or more qualifying children, he or she may calculate the additional child tax credit according to his or her portion of Social Security and Medicare taxes greater than the earned income credit, though this cannot be greater than the amount of the child tax credit left over after the regular and alternative minimum taxes are decreased to zero. Taxpayers with three or more qualifying children should only use this alternate method of calculation if it results in a greater credit.

Educational credits

Some taxpayers may receive a Lifetime Learning Credit or an American Opportunity Tax Credit for the costs of postsecondary education. The maximum Lifetime Learning Credit was $2,000 in 2015. This tax credit is not refundable, but it may be claimed for any higher education. The American Opportunity Tax Credit, on the other hand, may only be claimed for the first four years of higher education. In 2015, 40 percent of the American Opportunity Tax Credit was refundable, meaning that taxpayers could receive credit in excess of their tax liability. However, the amount of the American Opportunity Tax Credit is reduced for taxpayers with a high modified adjusted gross income. Neither of these educational credits can be claimed by a married taxpayer filing separately. These credits only apply to qualified expenses for the taxpayer, a dependent, or his or her spouse.

Requirements for receiving a Lifetime Learning Credit or an American Opportunity Tax Credit

In order to receive the Lifetime Learning Credit or the American Opportunity Tax Credit, taxpayers must be citizens or residents of the United States. If the taxpayer is married, he or she must file jointly. Taxpayers may only claim an educational credit for dependents who are claimed as an exemption on their tax return as well. Also, the monetary value of qualified expenses used to calculate the educational credit will be diminished by any scholarships not subject to taxation. Money that is received as a gift, loan, inheritance, or savings withdrawal does not decrease the amount of qualified expenses. However, untaxed distributions from 529 plans (otherwise known as qualified tuition programs) do reduce qualified expenses. Taxpayers may not both claim an educational credit and take a deduction for tuition and fees. Taxpayers should select the strategy that results in the greatest benefit. Taxpayers may not claim both the American Opportunity Tax Credit and the Lifetime Learning Credit for the same student.

American Opportunity Tax Credit

The American Opportunity Tax Credit may be applied to the entirety of the first $2,000 of qualified educational expenses and a quarter of the next $2,000 of qualified expenses. In other words, the maximum credit is $2,500. The taxpayer may have 40 percent of the American Opportunity Tax Credit refunded, and may obtain this credit for four years after high school. There are modified adjusted gross income limits for this credit: for taxpayers filing as single, head of household, or qualifying widow, the credit begins phasing out at $80,000 of modified adjusted gross income, and the taxpayer becomes ineligible at $90,000; for married taxpayers filing jointly, phase-out begins at $160,000 and ends at $180,000. This credit may not be claimed for any student with a felony drug conviction. Although students are only able to claim this credit four times, if postsecondary education takes longer than four years it may be possible for the same student to claim a Lifetime Learning Credit for the extra years. The only expenses that qualify for the American Opportunity Tax Credit are tuition and fees.

Lifetime Learning Credit

The Lifetime Learning Credit reimburses the taxpayer for 20 percent of the first $10,000 paid for all eligible students. In other words, the maximum amount of the credit is $2,000 per taxpayer, not per student. This credit is not refundable, unlike the American Opportunity Tax Credit, and it is subject to modified adjusted gross income limitations. Taxpayers who file as a single, head of household, or qualifying widow will have their Lifetime Learning Credit phased out at MAGI of $51,000, and will become ineligible for the credit at $61,000. Married taxpayers who file jointly will have the credit phased out at

$102,000, and will become ineligible for the credit at $122,000. The Lifetime Learning Credit may be applied to any post-secondary educational program, even when the student is not pursuing a particular degree or credential. The credit may be applied to tuition, fees, books, and school supplies.

Credit for qualified retirement savings contributions

The Internal Revenue Service offers a qualified retirement savings contribution credit to promote the growth of IRAs and 401(k) plans. Taxpayers are eligible to receive this credit in addition to the tax deduction associated with their contributions. In order to obtain the qualified retirement savings contribution, the taxpayer must add money to a traditional IRA, Roth IRA, 401(k), 403(b), or qualified 4974(c) retirement plan. The contribution to an IRA cannot be a rollover contribution, and the contribution to a 401(k) or 403(b) plan must be an elective deferral. A taxpayer may not claim this credit if he was born in 1994 or after, if he was claimed as a dependent by another taxpayer, or if he is a full-time student.

Modified adjusted gross income threshold for the qualified retirement savings contribution credit

There is a modified adjusted gross income threshold for the qualified retirement savings contribution credit: in 2015, married taxpayers filing jointly were eligible for a credit equal to 50 percent of their contribution if they made less than $36,500; however, married taxpayers filing jointly were ineligible for the deduction if they made over $61,000. Taxpayers filing as a head of household were eligible for the full credit if they made $27,375 or less, but could not receive the credit if they made more than $45,750. All other taxpayers could claim the full 50 percent credit if they made $18,250 or less, but could claim no credit if they made more than $30,500. The amount of the credit is calculated on Form 8880, *Credit for Qualified Retirement Savings Contributions*, which may accompany Form 1040 or 1040 A.

Nonbusiness energy property credit

Taxpayers may be eligible for a nonrefundable credit for improvements to the energy system of a nonbusiness property. In 2015, the credit was 30 percent of qualifying expenses, though specific improvements could only receive a maximum credit of $500. Moreover, improvements involving windows were only eligible for a maximum lifetime credit of $200. Any previous energy-related credit for nonbusiness property reduces the amount of the credit that can be claimed in subsequent years. It is uncertain whether this credit will be available in the future. Some of the improvement expenses that may be eligible for the credit are related to insulation, roofing, doors, and HVAC systems. Some of these improvements are subject to the same dollar limitations as improvements involving windows.

Residential energy-efficient property credit

Taxpayers may be eligible for a residential energy efficient property credit for the expenses related to promoting green technologies in the home. For instance, a taxpayer may be able to receive a benefit for adding solar energy technology. This benefit may reimburse the taxpayer not only for the cost of the equipment, but also for expenses related to labor, installation, and maintenance. If the taxpayer claims a residential energy credit on his or her tax return, then the taxpayer's basis in the property is diminished by that amount. Residential energy efficient property credits are claimed on Form 5695, *Residential Energy Credits*, which may accompany only Form 1040.

Credits available for elderly or disabled taxpayers

There is a nonrefundable tax credit available for elderly and disabled taxpayers. This credit is only available for taxpayers who are at least 65 or who are retired on full disability with a taxable disability income. Full disability means that the taxpayer is totally and permanently disabled, incapable of gainful employment. Married taxpayers who file separately are not eligible to claim this credit unless they did not live in the same household as their spouse at any time during the year. There is also a limit for this credit based on income, though either adjusted gross income or nontaxable pensions/Social Security benefits may be counted. For instance, in 2015 taxpayers who filed as single, head of household, or qualifying widow with dependent child could not claim the credit for the elderly or the disabled if their adjusted gross income was $17,500 or more, or if they received $5,000 or more of nontaxable pension/Social Security benefits. The amount of the credit is calculated on Schedule R, *Credit for the Elderly or the Disabled*, which may not be attached to Form 1040 EZ.

Foreign tax credit

When a taxpayer is required to pay foreign income taxes, he or she may either take an itemized deduction or a nonrefundable tax credit on the amount of the tax. Taxpayers are allowed to choose the option that provides the greater tax benefit. In order to claim the foreign tax credit, the taxpayer must complete Form 1116, unless all of the foreign income and tax was reported on Forms 1099-INT and 1099-DIV, all of the foreign income was passive, the total amount of foreign taxes did not exceed $300 ($600 for married couples filing jointly), and the taxpayer would prefer to claim the foreign tax credit on the return. If the taxpayer claims the foreign tax credit on Form 1116, the credit may not exceed the product of domestic tax liability multiplied by foreign taxable income divided by total taxable income.

Mortgage interest credit

There is a nonrefundable tax credit available for the mortgage interest of homeowners who make less than a certain amount of money. Taxpayers may be eligible for this mortgage interest credit if they have received a qualified mortgage credit certificate from the state or local government: this certificate indicates the mortgage value the taxpayer may not exceed in order to receive the credit. If the taxpayer's mortgage loan amount is greater than the value on the qualified mortgage credit certificate, the taxpayer may only obtain a partial credit. The amount of the credit is calculated by dividing the amount of certified indebtedness indicated on the mortgage credit certificate by the original amount of the mortgage, and then multiplying the quotient by the total amount of mortgage interest paid during the year. This amount is multiplied by the credit certificate rate to determine the credit value if the certificate credit rate is 20 percent or less. If the certified credit rate is 20 percent or greater, the maximum credit is $2,000.

Adoption credit

Taxpayers who adopt a child are eligible for a refundable tax credit. An adopted child qualifies for this tax credit if he or she is either 17 years of age or younger, or is disabled. This credit can be used to reimburse the taxpayer's expenses for adoption, court fees, legal fees, travel expenses, and the re-adoption expenses associated with taking in a child from another country. As with other tax credits, there is a modified adjusted gross income limitation for the adoption credit. Taxpayers may claim the entire credit if their modified adjusted gross income is $185,210 or less. If modified adjusted gross income is greater than $225,210, the taxpayer becomes ineligible for the adoption credit. This credit should be claimed for the year in which the adoption is finalized, though in some cases a taxpayer may be able to claim the credit for an adoption that is never finalized and never actually occurs. The adoption credit is reported on Form 8839, which may only be attached to Form 1040.

Homebuyer credit

Taxpayers who purchased their first home before May 1, 2010, may be eligible for a refundable homebuyer tax credit. Specifically, this credit is still available for members of the armed services, the intelligence community, or the Foreign Service. In order to receive this credit, the taxpayer must have served qualified official extended duty abroad for a minimum of 90 days between the beginning of 2009 and April 30, 2010. The amount of the credit is either 10 percent of the price of the home or $8,000, whichever is smaller. As with other tax credits, the first-time homebuyer credit is subject to modified adjusted gross income limitations. If modified adjusted gross income is less than $125,000, the taxpayer may receive the full credit. If modified adjusted gross income is $145,000 or more, the taxpayer is ineligible for the credit. The modified adjusted gross income limitations are slightly higher for married couples filing jointly. Also, taxpayers may not claim this credit if they purchased their home from a relative, if the home cost more than $800,000, if they were younger than 18 when they purchased the home, or if they were claimed as a dependent by another taxpayer.

Health coverage tax credit

Some taxpayers may be eligible for a tax credit for health coverage expenses incurred after being displaced from their job. The health coverage tax credit is refundable, and is calculated for individual months. Beginning in July 2015, the amount of the credit was 72.5 percent of premiums. To be eligible for this tax credit, the taxpayer must be eligible for trade adjustment assistance, or must be the recipient of a Pension Benefit Guaranty Corporation pension. The taxpayer may not receive at least half of the expense of health coverage from his or her employer, and must pay his or her portion of premiums directly to the health plan. Also, in order to be eligible for this credit the taxpayer may not be the recipient of benefits from Medicaid, Medicare, the Children's Health Insurance Program, or the Federal Employees Health Benefits Program. The health coverage tax credit is claimed on Form 8885, which may only be attached to Form 1040.

Other Taxes

Calculation of regular tax liability

The calculation of regular income tax indicates the base amount of the taxpayer's liability, before consideration of the alternative minimum tax or tax credits. The calculation of regular tax liability begins with a summary of taxable income. Taxable income is calculated by finding gross income and then subtracting adjustments to gross income, either standard or itemized deductions, and personal and dependent exemptions. If taxable income is less than $100,000, the taxpayer may then compute his or her regular tax with the table provided by the IRS in Publication 17, *Your Federal Income Tax*. If taxable income is $100,000 or more, the taxpayer may compute his or her regular tax with a special tax rate worksheet, and may not use Form 1040 A or 1040 EZ.

After calculating the amount of regular tax, the full measure of tax liability is calculated by first adjusting for the amount of any alternative minimum tax. Next, the taxpayer will subtract the value of any tax credits for which he or she is eligible. After this, the taxpayer will add any extra taxes owed along with the regular tax or the alternative minimum tax. For instance, the taxpayer may owe a self-employment tax, a tax on household employees, or a penalty related to an individual retirement account. Finally, the taxpayer will subtract any tax payments that have already been made. For instance, the taxpayer may have paid part of his tax during a filing extension, or may have made estimated tax payments. Also, many taxpayers will have had taxes withheld from their wages. After this final calculation, the taxpayer should understand the amount he or she owes.

Special circumstances

There are special rules for taxing net long-term capital gains and qualified dividends. The maximum tax rate for these sources of income was 15 percent in 2015, and taxpayers who made less than a certain amount of money did not have to pay any tax at all. The taxpayer's specific degree of taxation is calculated with the *Qualified Dividends and Capital Gains Tax* Worksheet. Unrecaptured Section 1250 gain is subject to a 25 percent tax rate. Section 1202 gain and collectibles gains are subject to a 28 percent tax rate. There are also special rules for lump-sum distributions from qualified retirement plans received by taxpayers born before January 2, 1936. These taxpayers may either treat part of the distribution as a capital gain, in which case it is taxed at 20 percent, or may have the entire distribution taxed at the 10-year average rate.

Alternative minimum tax

The alternative minimum tax prevents high-income individuals from avoiding a reasonable amount of taxation. Taxpayers will become subject to the alternative minimum tax if they make a certain amount of money and have deductions or exclusions exceeding a certain amount. The extent of alternative minimum tax liability is calculated on Form 6251. To begin with, the taxpayer calculates his or her regular taxable income before the standard deduction and any personal exemptions. Then, the taxpayer enters any adjustments and preferences specific to the alternative minimum tax. The taxpayer then subtracts the amount of the alternative minimum tax exemption, and multiplies alternative minimum taxable income by either 26 percent or 28 percent, depending on whether income is less or more than $175,000, to produce tentative minimum tax liability. If this calculation produces a value greater than the regular tax, then the difference is the amount of alternative minimum tax, which is paid along with the regular tax.

<u>Typical triggers</u>
A taxpayer may be subject to the alternative minimum tax if he or she has a high enough income and certain deductions or exemptions. For instance, the standard deduction is not included in the calculation of alternative minimum tax, and neither are personal and dependency exemptions. State and local taxes are not deductible with respect to the alternative minimum tax. Unlike in the calculation of regular tax, the difference between stock and option price is considered income with respect to the alternative minimum tax. Also, the amount of home mortgage interest deducted is not considered for alternative minimum tax purposes if the mortgage was used to refinance another mortgage. Finally, interest on private activity municipal bonds is included in the calculation of alternative minimum tax, though it is exempt from gross income in the calculation of regular tax.

<u>Calculating</u>
The procedure for calculating the alternative minimum tax depends on whether the taxpayer has itemized deductions or claimed the standard deduction. If the taxpayer has itemized deduction, the calculation of the alternative minimum tax begins with taxable income with respect to the regular tax; if the taxpayer claimed the standard deduction, the calculation of the alternative minimum tax begins with adjusted gross income. Whichever amount is used, it is adjusted by deferral items: tax preference items increase the alternative minimum taxable income, and adjustment items decrease it. For instance, there are different depreciation standards for the alternative minimum tax. Also, personal and dependency exemptions may not be claimed for the purposes of the alternative minimum tax. Taxpayers are allowed to reduce the alternative minimum taxable income according to their filing status (the greatest exemptions are for taxpayers who are married filing jointly or qualifying widows). The exemption is diminished over certain levels of alternative minimum taxable income. The alternative minimum tax is then either 26 percent or 28 percent, depending on whether alternative minimum taxable income is less or more, respectively, than $175,000.

Kiddie tax

The kiddie tax is the name for the special rules for calculating the tax on the investment income of children. In the past, it was possible for wealthy parents to avoid paying taxes by placing some of their investment income in the names of their children. The kiddie tax only applies to certain sources of unearned income. It applies when the child's investment income exceeds a threshold amount, adjusted for inflation. Also, the child must be either under the age of 18 or a full-time student under the age of 24. The amount of kiddie tax owed is reported on Form 8615, *Tax for Certain Children Who Have Investment Income of More Than $1900*. The types of income that may be eligible for this tax are capital gains, dividends, trust distributions, capital gains distributions, taxable interest, and the taxable portion of pension or Social Security benefits. It is important to note that a child does not need to be a dependent in order to be subject to the kiddie tax.

Completion of the Filing Process

Recording tax payments and withholdings

In order to get credit for tax payments and withholdings made during the year, the taxpayer must keep accurate and comprehensive records. For instance, the taxpayer must record any estimated taxes that have been paid, as well as any withholdings on wages and supplemental compensation. The taxpayer must record any tax refunds from previous years that have been applied towards the present tax liability, and must indicate the mandatory 20 percent withholding on lump-sum distributions from qualified retirement plans, as well as any optional withholdings and distributions from IRAs or other qualified plans. The taxpayer must record any optional withholdings from unemployment or Social Security benefits, and must note any backup withholding on interest or dividends.

Paying the tax balance

When the taxpayer has not made sufficient tax payments to absorb his or her tax liability, he or she will owe the balance. A taxpayer may pay his or her balance by check, money order, direct debit, credit card, or the Electronic Federal Tax Payment System (EFTPS). Checks should be made out to the United States Treasury, and should be accompanied by Form 1040-V, *Payment Voucher*. The taxpayer should write his or her Social Security number and the version of the return he or she is filing on the check. When a taxpayer elects to pay by direct debit, he or she must give the routing and account numbers. The IRS allows payment through major credit cards without a fee, though most card providers do charge a small fee for tax payments. Finally, taxpayers who have previously registered at EFTPS.gov may use the Electronic Federal Tax Payment System to transfer funds from their bank account to the U.S. Treasury.

Insufficient funds to cover tax liability

The IRS has established some solutions for taxpayers who are unable to pay their full liability at the time it is due. For instance, if the taxpayer can demonstrate that making a full payment by the deadline would create undue hardship, he or she may receive a short-term extension, typically about 120 days. Some taxpayers receive a short-term extension that is as long as six months. The taxpayer's liability will continue to accrue interest until it is paid off. Another option for taxpayers with insufficient funds is to file Form 1127, *Application for Extension of Time for Payment of Tax Due to Undue Hardship*. This form must be accompanied by a statement indicating the taxpayer's assets and liabilities. If this form is approved, the taxpayer will receive a short-term extension, during which his or her tax liability will continue to accrue interest at the federal short-term rate plus 3 percent.

Paying off a tax liability in installments

Any taxpayer may receive permission to discharge his or her tax liability in installments, provided he or she has filed all the necessary paperwork and has an overall tax liability of less than $25,000. An installment agreement is requested with Form 9465. The typical agreement requires the taxpayer to make good on his or her debt within a period of 36 to

60 months. For taxpayers who owe more than $25,000, installment agreements are not guaranteed, and require the filing of Form 9465 and Form 433-F, *Collection Information Statement*. There is a small fee associated with installment payments, though the fee is reduced if the taxpayer agrees to a direct debit withdrawal of funds. This fee is added to the overall tax liability. It should be noted that the tax liability continues to accrue interest and penalties for non-payment during an installment agreement.

Compromise offer to the IRS

If the taxpayer feels that he or she will be unable to make a full payment of his or her tax liability, he or she may make what is called an offer in compromise, or OIC. The IRS, however, will only approve an offer in compromise in certain situations. For instance, the IRS may approve such an offer if there is a reasonable doubt as to whether the taxpayer should be required to pay the money in the first place. Of course, the taxpayer will need to make a convincing case establishing this reasonable doubt. The taxpayer may also submit a compromise offer if payment of the tax would create an economic hardship, or could be reasonably described as unfair. Again, the taxpayer will need to submit adequate documentation to support this claim. Finally, a taxpayer may make an offer of compromise if he or she will not be able to pay the full amount before the expiration of the statute of limitations for collection.

Procedure
To make an offer in compromise in lieu of full payment of the tax liability, the taxpayer must submit Form 656 and either Form 433-A or Form 433-B. Along with Form 656, the taxpayer will need to pay a nonrefundable $150 fee. If the taxpayer is claiming that his or her liability is unjustified, he or she does not need to submit a down payment, but otherwise 20 percent of the offer in compromise is due with the submission of the offer. In order to have an offer in compromise approved, a taxpayer needs to file all of the relevant federal tax returns. Moreover, the taxpayer needs to have paid all of his or her estimated taxes during the present tax year. Taxpayers who are involved in an open audit or bankruptcy case may not make an offer in compromise.

Obtaining a tax refund

If the taxpayer is eligible for a refund, he or she may elect to receive it as a direct deposit or check from the United States Treasury, or may elect to have it applied to his or her future taxes. When the taxpayer selects direct deposit, he or she must indicate the account and routings number on the return. The Internal Revenue Service allows taxpayers to distribute a refund among several different accounts, though this requires the submission of Form 8888, *Allocation of Refund (including Savings Bond Purchases)*. Taxpayers may have a refund placed in a checking account, savings account, health savings account, Archer medical savings account, individual retirement account, Coverdell education savings account, or Treasury Direct online account. The taxpayer is responsible for ensuring that the account to which he or she directs the refund will be ready to receive it.

Handling problems with refunds

If the taxpayer elects to have his or her refund issued through direct deposit, it may arrive within two to three weeks after the return is filed. If the taxpayer prefers to receive a check from the United States Treasury, it will usually arrive within a month and a half of the filing deadline. If the refund is not issued within a month and a half of the filing deadline, the taxpayer is eligible for interest. Moreover, if the taxpayer submits an amended return and is eligible for a greater refund, he or she may be able to receive interest payments on this as well. If the taxpayer claims a refund but owes child support, a student loan, or federal or state income taxes from the previous year, the refund may be withheld. Married people filing jointly may have their refund withheld if one spouse has outstanding debt. However, if the other spouse feels that he or she has been wrongly denied a refund, it is possible to make an appeal through Form 8379, *Injured Spouse Allocation*.

Payment of estimated taxes

When the taxpayer anticipates owing at least $1,000 during a tax year, accounting for refundable tax credits and withholdings, he or she is required to pay estimated taxes. Estimated taxes are paid every quarter, in amounts calculated on the estimated tax worksheet accompanying Form 1040-ES. The taxpayer may adjust his or her estimated tax payments during the year if he or she has some tax money withheld or becomes eligible for deductions or tax credits. However, if the taxpayer pays too little estimated taxes, he or she may be penalized. The penalty is calculated on Form 2210. There are three different methods for calculating whether the estimated tax has been underpaid; the taxpayer will need to select the method that is appropriate for his or her situation. If the taxpayer failed to make an estimated payment because of a casualty or disaster, or if the taxpayer became disabled or retired during the year, he or she may be exempt from the penalty.

Accrual of interest on an unpaid tax liability

If the taxpayer fails to pay some or all of his or her liability, interest may accrue. A taxpayer may be charged interest on any amount of tax that is not received by the filing due date. Receiving an extension does not preclude the accrual of interest. When the taxpayer pays more money than he or she should, he or she may receive interest payments from the IRS. The rate of interest is established by the Internal Revenue Service and adjusted every quarter. If the taxpayer can prove that partial or full nonpayment was the result of an error by the IRS, he or she may be able to have the interest charges decreased or eliminated.

Penalty for late filing or late payment of taxes

In most cases, a taxpayer will be penalized 5 percent of his or her outstanding tax liability for each month or part of a month in which the return is unfiled. However, the maximum penalty for late filing is 25 percent. The penalty for failing to pay is significantly smaller. A taxpayer will be charged 0.5 percent of his or her tax liability for each month or part of the month following the due date. If the taxpayer has paid at least 90 percent of what he or she owes before the original due date, there is no penalty for failure to pay the rest on time. If the IRS is forced to issue a demand for immediate payment, the penalty for failing to pay will immediately increase to 1 percent per month. If the taxpayer is subject to a penalty for both failing to file and failing to pay, the penalty related to late filing will be diminished by the value of the penalty for late paying.

Penalties for inaccurate statements or frivolous tax returns

If the taxpayer makes inaccurate statements on his or her tax return, he or she may be penalized 20 percent of any resulting underpayment. If the taxpayer can demonstrate that his or her inaccurate statements were based on faulty IRS rulings or court decisions, he or she may be able to avoid the penalty. If the taxpayer files a frivolous return or includes frivolous information, meaning that there is not enough detail to calculate the tax liability or the detail included is clearly wrong, he or she may be subject to a $5,000 penalty. Married taxpayers filing jointly may be subject to two $5,000 penalties, one for each spouse. If the check written to the Internal Revenue Service bounces, the taxpayer will be penalized 2 percent of the check's value. The only exception to this is if the check is for an amount below $1,250, in which case the penalty is either $25 or the entire value of the check, whichever is smaller.

Protocol for finishing a tax return

Before the tax return is filed, the taxpayer needs to ensure that his or her name, taxpayer identification number, and date of birth are accurate. The taxpayer should also verify the accuracy of all the information entered on the form. When filing, taxpayers should be sure to receive a proof of filing, which is some form of acknowledgment from the IRS or U.S. Postal Service. If necessary, the taxpayer should request an automatic six-month extension with Form 4868. Finally, when filing a tax return the taxpayer should be sure to retain a copy of the return and any other important documents, such as receipts, bank statements, checks, and invoices. Most tax professionals recommend keeping a copy of the return and any other important records for at least three years after filing.

Signing the tax return

In order to be considered official by the Internal Revenue Service, a tax return must be signed by the taxpayer. The taxpayer's signature indicates that the information on the return is complete and accurate. If the taxpayer is using a third party to help file his or her return, he or she must indicate as much on the return. This gives the third party permission to supply the IRS with any additional documentation or clarification that becomes necessary. The third party must sign the returns and give his or her preparer tax identification number. Moreover, a third-party tax preparer must supply the name of his or her employer, as well as full contact information and an employer identification number. If the taxpayer dies before the filing of the return and is therefore unable to sign, his or her appointed personal representative should affix a signature. If there is no appointed personal representative, the surviving spouse or the caretaker of the taxpayer's property may sign.

Claiming innocent spouse relief

If the IRS declares a tax liability for one spouse, and the other spouse believes he or she should be exempt from this liability, that spouse may apply for innocent spouse relief. Basic innocent spouse relief is available for those whose spouse has entered incorrect information on the return, or for those for whom the tax liability would be unfair. A spouse may receive separation of liability relief if he or she is legally separated from his partner, and is therefore not responsible for the tax liability. An innocent spouse may receive equitable relief when he or she is able to demonstrate special circumstances. All of the information related to this subject is contained in IRS Publication 971, *Innocent Spouse Relief*.

E-filing mandates for registered tax preparers

When a tax preparer is planning on filing more than 10 returns for individuals, estates, and trusts, he or she must submit these returns electronically. It takes about a month and a half to become an authorized e-filer. Each client of the tax preparer should be told that his or her return will be filed electronically, and should be given an option to decline the service. Taxpayers should be aware that e-filing results in a faster refund and a more secure transmission of information. If the taxpayer declines to have his or her return filed electronically, the tax preparer may submit a paper return. Amended returns and returns for nonresident aliens may not be filed electronically. In addition, taxpayers may not e-file returns that claim the adoption credit. In order to e-file, the taxpayer will need to obtain a self-select PIN or a practitioner PIN. When the tax preparer files a return electronically, he or she is responsible for giving the taxpayer a copy of the return.

Practices and Procedures

Penalties for improper e-filing

The tax preparer who violates the rules of e-filing may be subject to sanction from the Internal Revenue Service. There are three levels of sanction. A Level One violation is one that has no substantial impact on the veracity of the return. Level I violations only receive a written reprimand. A Level Two violation negatively affects the quality of the return, and is therefore subject to a more significant penalty. For instance, the IRS may suspend the tax preparer for one year following the sanction. A Level Three violation is one that significantly affects the quality of the return. A tax preparer who commits a Level Three violation may be suspended for two years or permanently expelled from the e-file system. It is possible for a tax preparer to appeal sanctions levied by the IRS.

Levels of authorization a taxpayer may grant to a tax preparer

A taxpayer may authorize his or her taxpayer to act as a liaison with the Internal Revenue Service. If the taxpayer grants power of attorney and makes a declaration of representative, he or she is essentially giving the tax preparer the authority to do anything the taxpayer would be able to do on his or her own behalf. For instance, a taxpayer who grants this authority gives the tax preparer the right to sign any documents and give any consent requested by the IRS. If the taxpayer gives the preparer tax information authorization, then the tax preparer has the right to obtain confidential information about the taxpayer from the IRS. If the taxpayer gives the tax preparer limited authorization as a third-party designee, then he or she is merely giving the tax preparer the authority to correspond with the IRS regarding the tax return. For instance, the tax preparer may have the authority to respond to requests for more information or for clarification.

Client confidentiality

Tax preparers are required to maintain a comprehensive list of the places where information about taxpayers is filed. The tax preparer is also required to monitor his or her filing systems to ensure against breaches of privacy. For instance, the tax preparer is required to take reasonable steps to avoid being hacked or having documents stolen. As part of this self-assessment, the tax preparer needs to consider the possible consequences of security breaches. The tax preparer needs to have an explicit plan for securing confidential information, and must update this plan as necessary. There are extensive details about this process in IRS Publication 4600, *Safeguarding Taxpayer Information*. If the tax preparer fails to take reasonable steps to ensure confidentiality, he or she may be subject to civil or criminal penalties.

Section 6694 penalties

If the tax preparer understates the client's tax liability, the preparer may be penalized by the IRS under Section 6694. The penalties depend on whether the tax preparer understated the liability on purpose. If the IRS determines that the tax preparer understated the liability due to reckless or intentional conduct, he or she may be subject to a penalty of $5,000 or 50 percent of the income earned from the client, whichever is higher. If the tax preparer understated liability unintentionally, but because he or she made an error or an unreasonable decision, the penalty will be either $1,000 or half of the income earned from the client, whichever is higher. The IRS will be especially concerned with seeing whether the tax preparer had a reasonable basis for the inaccurate statement, and whether he or she had a substantial authority to make the statement.

Section 6695 penalties

Section 6695 of the Internal Revenue Code outlines the penalties for failure to perform certain essential tasks as a tax preparer. For instance, if the tax preparer fails to sign the return, he or she will be subject to a penalty of $50 for each failure. Similarly, the tax preparer will be penalized $50 for each time he or she fails to provide the taxpayer with a completed copy of the return, fails to provide a preparer tax identification number, fails to maintain a list of taxpayer names and identification numbers, or fails to file the correct information returns. The total for each of these penalties cannot exceed $25,000 in a calendar year. If the tax preparer deposits a client's refund check in his or her personal account, he or she will be penalized $500 for each check. If the taxpayer does not perform due diligence in the assessment of the client's eligibility for the earned income tax credit, he or she will be fined $500 for each failure. With respect to the earned income tax credit, due diligence is defined as the completion of Form 8867, *Paid Preparer Earned Income Credit Checklist*.

Ethics

Circular 230

Circular 230 identifies the people who are eligible to represent taxpayers in their dealings with the Department of the Treasury. The standards of conduct are established by the Office of Professional Responsibility and the Return Preparer Office, both of which are divisions of the Internal Revenue Service. According to Circular 230, the following professionals are allowed to represent taxpayers: enrolled retirement plan agents; enrolled actuaries; enrolled agents; certified public accountants; attorneys; and registered tax return preparers. In limited circumstances, supervised preparers and non-Form 1040 series preparers are allowed to represent taxpayers. A supervised preparer works for an authorized preparer, but does not sign tax returns. Registered tax return preparers are restricted with regards to the advice they can give clients, as well as the IRS officers with whom they are allowed to correspond.

Sections 10.20, 10.22, 10.23, and 10.24

According to Section 10.20 of Circular 230, a registered tax return preparer is required to let clients know when they have not provided enough information or have made an error on their tax return or a related document. The tax preparer is required to explain the omission or error completely, including any possible penalties that may result from it. According to Section 10.22 of Circular 230, a registered tax return preparer must exercise due diligence in the preparation and filing of all tax forms, as well as in all of his or her correspondence with the IRS and Department of the Treasury. In some cases, this will require the registered tax return preparer to request additional information from the taxpayer. According to Section 10.23, a registered tax return preparer may not delay the settling of any matter with the IRS without reason. According to Section 10.24, a registered tax return preparer may not consciously accept assistance from a person who has been disbarred or suspended by the IRS.

Sections 10.25 through 10.30

Section 10.25 of Circular 230 asserts that a taxpayer may not be assisted by a former government employee if this assistance would violate federal law. According to Section 10.26, a taxpayer is not allowed to act as a notary on any matter in which he or she has an interest. According to Section 10.27, a registered tax return preparer is not allowed to charge unconscionable fees for his or her services, meaning that the tax preparer may not make exorbitant or outrageous claims against his or her clients. Section 10.28 of Circular 230 states that a tax preparer must return client records promptly upon request. Section 10.29 states that a registered tax return preparer may not engage in professional services when it would create a conflict of interest. This means that a taxpayer should not engage in any professional activity in which his representation to one party would be limited by his responsibility to another. Section 10.30 of Circular 230 states that registered tax return preparers may not advertise with fraudulent, false, or coercive statements, and may not imply to potential customers that they are employed by the IRS.

<u>Sections 10.31 through 10.37</u>
Section 10.31 of Circular 230 states that a registered tax return preparer may not endorse or negotiate any check issued by clients to pay off a tax liability. Section 10.32 states that tax preparers are not authorized to practice law in any form. Section 10.33 states that tax preparers are obliged to follow best practices, including clear communication with clients and consistent honesty in communications with the IRS. Section 10.34 states that tax preparers may not intentionally or through negligence make unreasonable claims or understate tax liability on the tax return. Section 10.35 outlines the type of advice a registered tax return preparer may provide. Section 10.36 states that a registered tax return preparer who oversees a team of other tax preparers must take reasonable steps to ensure compliance with Circular 230 by all employees. Finally, Section 10.37 outlines the types of written advice that a registered tax return preparer may give to clients.

<u>Sections 10.50 through 10.53</u>
According to Section 10.50 of Circular 230, the Internal Revenue Service may sanction registered tax return preparers for incompetence, disreputable conduct, violations, or intentional defrauding, misleading, or threatening of clients. Sanctions may include public censure, suspension, or disbarment. According to Section 10.51, a registered tax return preparer may be sanctioned for incompetence and disreputable conduct if he or she is convicted of any federal crime, felony, or criminal offense involving dishonesty. A tax preparer may also be sanctioned in this manner for intentionally or through negligence making dishonest statements on the tax return. Section 10.52 states that tax preparers may be sanctioned for any violation of Circular 230. According to Section 10.53, IRS employees who suspect that a tax preparer has committed a violation must immediately report it in writing.

Eligibility requirements for registered tax return preparers

In order to become a registered tax return preparer, one must be at least 18 years old, must have a valid preparer tax identification number, must have a clean record of conduct, and must pass a written examination. Tax return preparers are required to file an application and pay a $30 fee every three years. They are also required to undergo a background check, which will include a close examination of the applicant's tax history. A registered taxpayer must renew his or her status every year on Form 8554. There are continuing education requirements for these professionals, including mandatory annual ethics training. Registered tax return preparers must maintain these continuing education records for four years after their certificate is renewed.

Secret Key #1 - Time is Your Greatest Enemy

Pace Yourself

Wear a watch. At the beginning of the test, check the time (or start a chronometer on your watch to count the minutes), and check the time after every few questions to make sure you are "on schedule."

If you are forced to speed up, do it efficiently. Usually one or more answer choices can be eliminated without too much difficulty. Above all, don't panic. Don't speed up and just begin guessing at random choices. By pacing yourself, and continually monitoring your progress against your watch, you will always know exactly how far ahead or behind you are with your available time. If you find that you are one minute behind on the test, don't skip one question without spending any time on it, just to catch back up. Take 15 fewer seconds on the next four questions, and after four questions you'll have caught back up. Once you catch back up, you can continue working each problem at your normal pace.

Furthermore, don't dwell on the problems that you were rushed on. If a problem was taking up too much time and you made a hurried guess, it must be difficult. The difficult questions are the ones you are most likely to miss anyway, so it isn't a big loss. It is better to end with more time than you need than to run out of time.

Lastly, sometimes it is beneficial to slow down if you are constantly getting ahead of time. You are always more likely to catch a careless mistake by working more slowly than quickly, and among very high-scoring test takers (those who are likely to have lots of time left over), careless errors affect the score more than mastery of material.

Secret Key #2 - Guessing is not Guesswork

You probably know that guessing is a good idea. Unlike other standardized tests, there is no penalty for getting a wrong answer. Even if you have no idea about a question, you still have a 20-25% chance of getting it right.

Most test takers do not understand the impact that proper guessing can have on their score. Unless you score extremely high, guessing will significantly contribute to your final score.

Monkeys Take the Test

What most test takers don't realize is that to insure that 20-25% chance, you have to guess randomly. If you put 20 monkeys in a room to take this test, assuming they answered once per question and behaved themselves, on average they would get 20-25% of the questions correct. Put 20 test takers in the room, and the average will be much lower among guessed questions. Why?
1. The test writers intentionally write deceptive answer choices that "look" right. A test taker has no idea about a question, so he picks the "best looking" answer, which is often wrong. The monkey has no idea what looks good and what doesn't, so it will consistently be right about 20-25% of the time.
2. Test takers will eliminate answer choices from the guessing pool based on a hunch or intuition. Simple but correct answers often get excluded, leaving a 0% chance of being correct. The monkey has no clue, and often gets lucky with the best choice.

This is why the process of elimination endorsed by most test courses is flawed and detrimental to your performance. Test takers don't guess; they make an ignorant stab in the dark that is usually worse than random.

$5 Challenge

Let me introduce one of the most valuable ideas of this course—the $5 challenge:

You only mark your "best guess" if you are willing to bet $5 on it.
You only eliminate choices from guessing if you are willing to bet $5 on it.

Why $5? Five dollars is an amount of money that is small yet not insignificant, and can really add up fast (20 questions could cost you $100). Likewise, each answer choice on one question of the test will have a small impact on your overall score, but it can really add up to a lot of points in the end.

The process of elimination IS valuable. The following shows your chance of guessing it right:

If you eliminate wrong answer choices until only this many remain:	Chance of getting it correct:
1	100%
2	50%
3	33%

However, if you accidentally eliminate the right answer or go on a hunch for an incorrect answer, your chances drop dramatically—to 0%. By guessing among all the answer choices, you are GUARANTEED to have a shot at the right answer.

That's why the $5 test is so valuable. If you give up the advantage and safety of a pure guess, it had better be worth the risk.

What we still haven't covered is how to be sure that whatever guess you make is truly random. Here's the easiest way:

Always pick the first answer choice among those remaining.

Such a technique means that you have decided, **before you see a single test question**, exactly how you are going to guess, and since the order of choices tells you nothing about which one is correct, this guessing technique is perfectly random.

This section is not meant to scare you away from making educated guesses or eliminating choices; you just need to define when a choice is worth eliminating. The $5 test, along with a pre-defined random guessing strategy, is the best way to make sure you reap all of the benefits of guessing.

Secret Key #3 - Practice Smarter, Not Harder

Many test takers delay the test preparation process because they dread the awful amounts of practice time they think necessary to succeed on the test. We have refined an effective method that will take you only a fraction of the time.

There are a number of "obstacles" in the path to success. Among these are answering questions, finishing in time, and mastering test-taking strategies. All must be executed on the day of the test at peak performance, or your score will suffer. The test is a mental marathon that has a large impact on your future.

Just like a marathon runner, it is important to work your way up to the full challenge. So first you just worry about questions, and then time, and finally strategy:

Success Strategy

1. Find a good source for practice tests.
2. If you are willing to make a larger time investment, consider using more than one study guide. Often the different approaches of multiple authors will help you "get" difficult concepts.
3. Take a practice test with no time constraints, with all study helps, "open book." Take your time with questions and focus on applying strategies.
4. Take a practice test with time constraints, with all guides, "open book."
5. Take a final practice test without open material and with time limits.

If you have time to take more practice tests, just repeat step 5. By gradually exposing yourself to the full rigors of the test environment, you will condition your mind to the stress of test day and maximize your success.

Secret Key #4 - Prepare, Don't Procrastinate

Let me state an obvious fact: if you take the test three times, you will probably get three different scores. This is due to the way you feel on test day, the level of preparedness you have, and the version of the test you see. Despite the test writers' claims to the contrary, some versions of the test WILL be easier for you than others.

Since your future depends so much on your score, you should maximize your chances of success. In order to maximize the likelihood of success, you've got to prepare in advance. This means taking practice tests and spending time learning the information and test taking strategies you will need to succeed.

Never go take the actual test as a "practice" test, expecting that you can just take it again if you need to. Take all the practice tests you can on your own, but when you go to take the official test, be prepared, be focused, and do your best the first time!

Secret Key #5 - Test Yourself

Everyone knows that time is money. There is no need to spend too much of your time or too little of your time preparing for the test. You should only spend as much of your precious time preparing as is necessary for you to get the score you need.

Once you have taken a practice test under real conditions of time constraints, then you will know if you are ready for the test or not.

If you have scored extremely high the first time that you take the practice test, then there is not much point in spending countless hours studying. You are already there.

Benchmark your abilities by retaking practice tests and seeing how much you have improved. Once you consistently score high enough to guarantee success, then you are ready.

If you have scored well below where you need, then knuckle down and begin studying in earnest. Check your improvement regularly through the use of practice tests under real conditions. Above all, don't worry, panic, or give up. The key is perseverance!

Then, when you go to take the test, remain confident and remember how well you did on the practice tests. If you can score high enough on a practice test, then you can do the same on the real thing.

General Strategies

The most important thing you can do is to ignore your fears and jump into the test immediately. Do not be overwhelmed by any strange-sounding terms. You have to jump into the test like jumping into a pool—all at once is the easiest way.

Make Predictions

As you read and understand the question, try to guess what the answer will be. Remember that several of the answer choices are wrong, and once you begin reading them, your mind will immediately become cluttered with answer choices designed to throw you off. Your mind is typically the most focused immediately after you have read the question and digested its contents. If you can, try to predict what the correct answer will be. You may be surprised at what you can predict.

Quickly scan the choices and see if your prediction is in the listed answer choices. If it is, then you can be quite confident that you have the right answer. It still won't hurt to check the other answer choices, but most of the time, you've got it!

Answer the Question

It may seem obvious to only pick answer choices that answer the question, but the test writers can create some excellent answer choices that are wrong. Don't pick an answer just because it sounds right, or you believe it to be true. It MUST answer the question. Once you've made your selection, always go back and check it against the question and make sure that you didn't misread the question and that the answer choice does answer the question posed.

Benchmark

After you read the first answer choice, decide if you think it sounds correct or not. If it doesn't, move on to the next answer choice. If it does, mentally mark that answer choice. This doesn't mean that you've definitely selected it as your answer choice, it just means that it's the best you've seen thus far. Go ahead and read the next choice. If the next choice is worse than the one you've already selected, keep going to the next answer choice. If the next choice is better than the choice you've already selected, mentally mark the new answer choice as your best guess.

The first answer choice that you select becomes your standard. Every other answer choice must be benchmarked against that standard. That choice is correct until proven otherwise by another answer choice beating it out. Once you've decided that no other answer choice seems as good, do one final check to ensure that your answer choice answers the question posed.

Valid Information

Don't discount any of the information provided in the question. Every piece of information may be necessary to determine the correct answer. None of the information in the question is there to throw you off (while the answer choices will certainly have information to throw you off). If two seemingly unrelated topics are discussed, don't ignore either. You can be confident there is a relationship, or it wouldn't be included in the question, and you are probably going to have to determine what is that relationship to find the answer.

Avoid "Fact Traps"

Don't get distracted by a choice that is factually true. Your search is for the answer that answers the question. Stay focused and don't fall for an answer that is true but irrelevant. Always go back to the question and make sure you're choosing an answer that actually answers the question and is not just a true statement. An answer can be factually correct, but it MUST answer the question asked. Additionally, two answers can both be seemingly correct, so be sure to read all of the answer choices, and make sure that you get the one that BEST answers the question.

Milk the Question

Some of the questions may throw you completely off. They might deal with a subject you have not been exposed to, or one that you haven't reviewed in years. While your lack of knowledge about the subject will be a hindrance, the question itself can give you many clues that will help you find the correct answer. Read the question carefully and look for clues. Watch particularly for adjectives and nouns describing difficult terms or words that you don't recognize. Regardless of whether you completely understand a word or not, replacing it with a synonym, either provided or one you more familiar with, may help you to understand what the questions are asking. Rather than wracking your mind about specific detailed information concerning a difficult term or word, try to use mental substitutes that are easier to understand.

The Trap of Familiarity

Don't just choose a word because you recognize it. On difficult questions, you may not recognize a number of words in the answer choices. The test writers don't put "make-believe" words on the test, so don't think that just because you only recognize all the words in one answer choice that that answer choice must be correct. If you only recognize words in one answer choice, then focus on that one. Is it correct? Try your best to determine if it is correct. If it is, that's great. If not, eliminate it. Each word and answer choice you eliminate increases your chances of getting the question correct, even if you then have to guess among the unfamiliar choices.

Eliminate Answers

Eliminate choices as soon as you realize they are wrong. But be careful! Make sure you consider all of the possible answer choices. Just because one appears right, doesn't mean that the next one won't be even better! The test writers will usually put more than one good answer choice for every question, so read all of them. Don't worry if you are stuck between two that seem right. By getting down to just two remaining possible choices, your odds are now 50/50. Rather than wasting too much time, play the odds. You are guessing, but guessing wisely because you've been able to knock out some of the answer choices that you know are wrong. If you are eliminating choices and realize that the last answer choice you are left with is also obviously wrong, don't panic. Start over and consider each choice again. There may easily be something that you missed the first time and will realize on the second pass.

Tough Questions

If you are stumped on a problem or it appears too hard or too difficult, don't waste time. Move on! Remember though, if you can quickly check for obviously incorrect answer choices, your chances of guessing correctly are greatly improved. Before you completely give up, at least try to knock out a couple of possible answers. Eliminate what you can and then guess at the remaining answer choices before moving on.

Brainstorm

If you get stuck on a difficult question, spend a few seconds quickly brainstorming. Run through the complete list of possible answer choices. Look at each choice and ask yourself, "Could this answer the question satisfactorily?" Go through each answer choice and consider it independently of the others. By systematically going through all possibilities, you may find something that you would otherwise overlook. Remember though that when you get stuck, it's important to try to keep moving.

Read Carefully

Understand the problem. Read the question and answer choices carefully. Don't miss the question because you misread the terms. You have plenty of time to read each question thoroughly and make sure you understand what is being asked. Yet a happy medium must be attained, so don't waste too much time. You must read carefully, but efficiently.

Face Value

When in doubt, use common sense. Always accept the situation in the problem at face value. Don't read too much into it. These problems will not require you to make huge leaps of logic. The test writers aren't trying to throw you off with a cheap trick. If you have to go beyond creativity and make a leap of logic in order to have an answer choice answer the question, then you should look at the other answer choices. Don't overcomplicate the problem by creating theoretical relationships or explanations that will warp time or space. These are normal problems rooted in reality. It's just that the applicable relationship or explanation may not be readily apparent and you have to figure things out. Use your common sense to interpret anything that isn't clear.

Prefixes

If you're having trouble with a word in the question or answer choices, try dissecting it. Take advantage of every clue that the word might include. Prefixes and suffixes can be a huge help. Usually they allow you to determine a basic meaning. Pre- means before, post- means after, pro - is positive, de- is negative. From these prefixes and suffixes, you can get an idea of the general meaning of the word and try to put it into context. Beware though of any traps. Just because con- is the opposite of pro-, doesn't necessarily mean congress is the opposite of progress!

Hedge Phrases

Watch out for critical hedge phrases, led off with words such as "likely," "may," "can," "sometimes," "often," "almost," "mostly," "usually," "generally," "rarely," and "sometimes." Question writers insert these hedge phrases to cover every possibility. Often an answer choice will be wrong simply because it leaves no room for exception. Unless the situation calls for them, avoid answer choices that have definitive words like "exactly," and "always."

Switchback Words

Stay alert for "switchbacks." These are the words and phrases frequently used to alert you to shifts in thought. The most common switchback word is "but." Others include "although," "however," "nevertheless," "on the other hand," "even though," "while," "in spite of," "despite," and "regardless of."

New Information

Correct answer choices will rarely have completely new information included. Answer choices typically are straightforward reflections of the material asked about and will directly relate to the question. If a new piece of information is included in an answer choice that doesn't even seem to relate to the topic being asked about, then that answer choice is likely incorrect. All of the information needed to answer the question is usually provided for you in the question. You should not have to make guesses that are unsupported or choose answer choices that require unknown information that cannot be reasoned from what is given.

Time Management

On technical questions, don't get lost on the technical terms. Don't spend too much time on any one question. If you don't know what a term means, then odds are you aren't going to get much further since you don't have a dictionary. You should be able to immediately recognize whether or not you know a term. If you don't, work with the other clues that you have—the other answer choices and terms provided—but don't waste too much time trying to figure out a difficult term that you don't know.

Contextual Clues

Look for contextual clues. An answer can be right but not the correct answer. The contextual clues will help you find the answer that is most right and is correct. Understand the context in which a phrase or statement is made. This will help you make important distinctions.

Don't Panic

Panicking will not answer any questions for you; therefore, it isn't helpful. When you first see the question, if your mind goes blank, take a deep breath. Force yourself to mechanically go through the steps of solving the problem using the strategies you've learned.

Pace Yourself

Don't get clock fever. It's easy to be overwhelmed when you're looking at a page full of questions, your mind is full of random thoughts and feeling confused, and the clock is ticking down faster than you would like. Calm down and maintain the pace that you have set for yourself. As long as you are on track by monitoring your pace, you are guaranteed to have enough time for yourself. When you get to the last few minutes of the test, it may seem like you won't have enough time left, but if you only have as many questions as you should have left at that point, then you're right on track!

Answer Selection

The best way to pick an answer choice is to eliminate all of those that are wrong, until only one is left and confirm that is the correct answer. Sometimes though, an answer choice may immediately look right. Be careful! Take a second to make sure that the other choices are not equally obvious. Don't make a hasty mistake. There are only two times that you should stop before checking other answers. First is when you are positive that the answer choice you have selected is correct. Second is when time is almost out and you have to make a quick guess!

Check Your Work

Since you will probably not know every term listed and the answer to every question, it is important that you get credit for the ones that you do know. Don't miss any questions through careless mistakes. If at all possible, try to take a second to look back over your answer selection and make sure you've selected the correct answer choice and haven't made a costly careless mistake (such as marking an answer choice that you didn't mean to mark). The time it takes for this quick double check should more than pay for itself in caught mistakes.

Beware of Directly Quoted Answers

Sometimes an answer choice will repeat word for word a portion of the question or reference section. However, beware of such exact duplication. It may be a trap! More than likely, the correct choice will paraphrase or summarize a point, rather than being exactly the same wording.

Slang

Scientific sounding answers are better than slang ones. An answer choice that begins "To compare the outcomes…" is much more likely to be correct than one that begins "Because some people insisted…"

Extreme Statements

Avoid wild answers that throw out highly controversial ideas that are proclaimed as established fact. An answer choice that states the "process should used in certain situations, if…" is much more likely to be correct than one that states the "process should be discontinued completely." The first is a calm rational statement and doesn't even make a definitive, uncompromising stance, using a hedge word "if" to provide wiggle room, whereas the second choice is a radical idea and far more extreme.

Answer Choice Families

When you have two or more answer choices that are direct opposites or parallels, one of them is usually the correct answer. For instance, if one answer choice states "x increases" and another answer choice states "x decreases" or "y increases," then those two or three answer choices are very similar in construction and fall into the same family of answer choices. A family of answer choices consists of two or three answer choices, very similar in construction, but often with directly opposite meanings. Usually the correct answer choice will be in that family of answer choices. The "odd man out" or answer choice that doesn't seem to fit the parallel construction of the other answer choices is more likely to be incorrect.

How to Overcome Test Anxiety

The very nature of tests caters to some level of anxiety, nervousness, or tension, just as we feel for any important event that occurs in our lives. A little bit of anxiety or nervousness can be a good thing. It helps us with motivation, and makes achievement just that much sweeter. However, too much anxiety can be a problem, especially if it hinders our ability to function and perform.

"Test anxiety," is the term that refers to the emotional reactions that some test-takers experience when faced with a test or exam. Having a fear of testing and exams is based upon a rational fear, since the test-taker's performance can shape the course of an academic career. Nevertheless, experiencing excessive fear of examinations will only interfere with the test-taker's ability to perform and chance to be successful.

There are a large variety of causes that can contribute to the development and sensation of test anxiety. These include, but are not limited to, lack of preparation and worrying about issues surrounding the test.

Lack of Preparation

Lack of preparation can be identified by the following behaviors or situations:

Not scheduling enough time to study, and therefore cramming the night before the test or exam
Managing time poorly, to create the sensation that there is not enough time to do everything
Failing to organize the text information in advance, so that the study material consists of the entire text and not simply the pertinent information
Poor overall studying habits

Worrying, on the other hand, can be related to both the test taker, or many other factors around him/her that will be affected by the results of the test. These include worrying about:

Previous performances on similar exams, or exams in general
How friends and other students are achieving
The negative consequences that will result from a poor grade or failure

There are three primary elements to test anxiety. Physical components, which involve the same typical bodily reactions as those to acute anxiety (to be discussed below). Emotional factors have to do with fear or panic. Mental or cognitive issues concerning attention spans and memory abilities.

Physical Signals

There are many different symptoms of test anxiety, and these are not limited to mental and emotional strain. Frequently there are a range of physical signals that will let a test taker know that he/she is suffering from test anxiety. These bodily changes can include the following:

Perspiring
Sweaty palms
Wet, trembling hands
Nausea
Dry mouth
A knot in the stomach
Headache
Faintness
Muscle tension
Aching shoulders, back and neck
Rapid heart beat
Feeling too hot/cold

To recognize the sensation of test anxiety, a test-taker should monitor him/herself for the following sensations:

The physical distress symptoms as listed above
Emotional sensitivity, expressing emotional feelings such as the need to cry or laugh too much, or a sensation of anger or helplessness
A decreased ability to think, causing the test-taker to blank out or have racing thoughts that are hard to organize or control.

Though most students will feel some level of anxiety when faced with a test or exam, the majority can cope with that anxiety and maintain it at a manageable level. However, those who cannot are faced with a very real and very serious condition, which can and should be controlled for the immeasurable benefit of this sufferer.

Naturally, these sensations lead to negative results for the testing experience. The most common effects of test anxiety have to do with nervousness and mental blocking.

Nervousness

Nervousness can appear in several different levels:

The test-taker's difficulty, or even inability to read and understand the questions on the test
The difficulty or inability to organize thoughts to a coherent form
The difficulty or inability to recall key words and concepts relating to the testing questions (especially essays)
The receipt of poor grades on a test, though the test material was well known by the test taker

Conversely, a person may also experience mental blocking, which involves:

Blanking out on test questions
Only remembering the correct answers to the questions when the test has already finished.

Fortunately for test anxiety sufferers, beating these feelings, to a large degree, has to do with proper preparation. When a test taker has a feeling of preparedness, then anxiety will be dramatically lessened.

The first step to resolving anxiety issues is to distinguish which of the two types of anxiety are being suffered. If the anxiety is a direct result of a lack of preparation, this should be considered a normal reaction, and the anxiety level (as opposed to the test results) shouldn't be anything to worry about. However, if, when adequately prepared, the test-taker still panics, blanks out, or seems to overreact, this is not a fully rational reaction. While this can be considered normal too, there are many ways to combat and overcome these effects.

Remember that anxiety cannot be entirely eliminated, however, there are ways to minimize it, to make the anxiety easier to manage. Preparation is one of the best ways to minimize test anxiety. Therefore the following techniques are wise in order to best fight off any anxiety that may want to build.

To begin with, try to avoid cramming before a test, whenever it is possible. By trying to memorize an entire term's worth of information in one day, you'll be shocking your system, and not giving yourself a very good chance to absorb the information. This is an easy path to anxiety, so for those who suffer from test anxiety, cramming should not even be considered an option.

Instead of cramming, work throughout the semester to combine all of the material which is presented throughout the semester, and work on it gradually as the course goes by, making sure to master the main concepts first, leaving minor details for a week or so before the test.

To study for the upcoming exam, be sure to pose questions that may be on the examination, to gauge the ability to answer them by integrating the ideas from your texts, notes and lectures, as well as any supplementary readings.

If it is truly impossible to cover all of the information that was covered in that particular term, concentrate on the most important portions, that can be covered very well. Learn these concepts as best as possible, so that when the test comes, a goal can be made to use these concepts as presentations of your knowledge.

In addition to study habits, changes in attitude are critical to beating a struggle with test anxiety. In fact, an improvement of the perspective over the entire test-taking experience can actually help a test taker to enjoy studying and therefore improve the overall experience. Be certain not to overemphasize the significance of the grade - know that the result of the test is neither a reflection of self worth, nor is it a measure of intelligence; one grade will not predict a person's future success.

To improve an overall testing outlook, the following steps should be tried:

Keeping in mind that the most reasonable expectation for taking a test is to expect to try to demonstrate as much of what you know as you possibly can.
Reminding ourselves that a test is only one test; this is not the only one, and there will be others.
The thought of thinking of oneself in an irrational, all-or-nothing term should be avoided at all costs.
A reward should be designated for after the test, so there's something to look forward to. Whether it be going to a movie, going out to eat, or simply visiting friends, schedule it in advance, and do it no matter what result is expected on the exam.

Test-takers should also keep in mind that the basics are some of the most important things, even beyond anti-anxiety techniques and studying. Never neglect the basic social, emotional and biological needs, in order to try to absorb information. In order to best achieve, these three factors must be held as just as important as the studying itself.

Study Steps

Remember the following important steps for studying:

Maintain healthy nutrition and exercise habits. Continue both your recreational activities and social pass times. These both contribute to your physical and emotional well being.
Be certain to get a good amount of sleep, especially the night before the test, because when you're overtired you are not able to perform to the best of your best ability.
Keep the studying pace to a moderate level by taking breaks when they are needed, and varying the work whenever possible, to keep the mind fresh instead of getting bored. When enough studying has been done that all the material that can be learned has been learned, and the test taker is prepared for the test, stop studying and do something relaxing such as listening to music, watching a movie, or taking a warm bubble bath.

There are also many other techniques to minimize the uneasiness or apprehension that is experienced along with test anxiety before, during, or even after the examination. In fact, there are a great deal of things that can be done to stop anxiety from interfering with lifestyle and performance. Again, remember that anxiety will not be eliminated entirely, and it shouldn't be. Otherwise that "up" feeling for exams would not exist, and most of us depend on that sensation to perform better than usual. However, this anxiety has to be at a level that is manageable.

Of course, as we have just discussed, being prepared for the exam is half the battle right away. Attending all classes, finding out what knowledge will be expected on the exam, and knowing the exam schedules are easy steps to lowering anxiety. Keeping up with work will remove the need to cram, and efficient study habits will eliminate wasted time. Studying should be done in an ideal location for concentration, so that it is simple to become interested in the material and give it complete attention. A method such as SQ3R (Survey, Question, Read, Recite, Review) is a wonderful key to follow to make sure that the study habits are as effective as possible, especially in the case of learning from a textbook. Flashcards are great techniques for memorization. Learning to take good notes will mean that notes will be full of useful information, so that less sifting will need to be done to seek out what is pertinent for studying. Reviewing notes after class and then again on occasion will keep the information fresh in the mind. From notes that have been taken summary sheets and outlines can be made for simpler reviewing.

A study group can also be a very motivational and helpful place to study, as there will be a sharing of ideas, all of the minds can work together, to make sure that everyone understands, and the studying will be made more interesting because it will be a social occasion.

Basically, though, as long as the test-taker remains organized and self confident, with efficient study habits, less time will need to be spent studying, and higher grades will be achieved.

To become self confident, there are many useful steps. The first of these is "self talk." It has been shown through extensive research, that self-talk for students who suffer from test anxiety, should be well monitored, in order to make sure that it contributes to self confidence as opposed to sinking the student. Frequently the self talk of test-anxious students is negative or self-defeating, thinking that everyone else is smarter and faster, that they always mess up, and that if they don't do well, they'll fail the entire course. It is important to decreasing anxiety that awareness is made of self talk. Try writing any negative self thoughts and then disputing them with a positive statement instead. Begin self-encouragement as though it was a friend speaking. Repeat positive statements to help reprogram the mind to believing in successes instead of failures.

Helpful Techniques

Other extremely helpful techniques include:

Self-visualization of doing well and reaching goals
While aiming for an "A" level of understanding, don't try to "overprotect" by setting your expectations lower. This will only convince the mind to stop studying in order to meet the lower expectations.
Don't make comparisons with the results or habits of other students. These are individual factors, and different things work for different people, causing different results.
Strive to become an expert in learning what works well, and what can be done in order to improve. Consider collecting this data in a journal.
Create rewards for after studying instead of doing things before studying that will only turn into avoidance behaviors.
Make a practice of relaxing - by using methods such as progressive relaxation, self-hypnosis, guided imagery, etc - in order to make relaxation an automatic sensation.
Work on creating a state of relaxed concentration so that concentrating will take on the focus of the mind, so that none will be wasted on worrying.
Take good care of the physical self by eating well and getting enough sleep.
Plan in time for exercise and stick to this plan.

Beyond these techniques, there are other methods to be used before, during and after the test that will help the test-taker perform well in addition to overcoming anxiety.

Before the exam comes the academic preparation. This involves establishing a study schedule and beginning at least one week before the actual date of the test. By doing this, the anxiety of not having enough time to study for the test will be automatically eliminated. Moreover, this will make the studying a much more effective experience, ensuring that the learning will be an easier process. This relieves much undue pressure on the test-taker.

Summary sheets, note cards, and flash cards with the main concepts and examples of these main concepts should be prepared in advance of the actual studying time. A topic should never be eliminated from this process. By omitting a topic because it isn't expected to be on the test is only setting up the test-taker for anxiety should it actually appear on the exam. Utilize the course syllabus for laying out the topics that should be studied. Carefully go over the notes that were made in class, paying special attention to any of the issues that the professor took special care to emphasize while lecturing in class. In the textbooks, use the chapter review, or if possible, the chapter tests, to begin your review.

It may even be possible to ask the instructor what information will be covered on the exam, or what the format of the exam will be (for example, multiple choice, essay, free form, true-false). Additionally, see if it is possible to find out how many questions will be on the test. If a review sheet or sample test has been offered by the professor, make good use of it, above anything else, for the preparation for the test. Another great resource for getting to know the examination is reviewing tests from previous semesters. Use these tests to review, and aim to achieve a 100% score on each of the possible topics. With a few exceptions, the goal that you set for yourself is the highest one that you will reach.

Take all of the questions that were assigned as homework, and rework them to any other possible course material. The more problems reworked, the more skill and confidence will form as a result. When forming the solution to a problem, write out each of the steps. Don't simply do head work. By doing as many steps on paper as possible, much clarification and therefore confidence will be formed. Do this with as many homework problems as possible, before checking the answers. By checking the answer after each problem, a reinforcement will exist, that will not be on the exam. Study situations should be as exam-like as possible, to prime the test-taker's system for the experience. By waiting to check the answers at the end, a psychological advantage will be formed, to decrease the stress factor.

Another fantastic reason for not cramming is the avoidance of confusion in concepts, especially when it comes to mathematics. 8-10 hours of study will become one hundred percent more effective if it is spread out over a week or at least several days, instead of doing it all in one sitting. Recognize that the human brain requires time in order to assimilate new material, so frequent breaks and a span of study time over several days will be much more beneficial.

Additionally, don't study right up until the point of the exam. Studying should stop a minimum of one hour before the exam begins. This allows the brain to rest and put things in their proper order. This will also provide the time to become as relaxed as possible when going into the examination room. The test-taker will also have time to eat well and eat sensibly. Know that the brain needs food as much as the rest of the body. With enough food and enough sleep, as well as a relaxed attitude, the body and the mind are primed for success.

Avoid any anxious classmates who are talking about the exam. These students only spread anxiety, and are not worth sharing the anxious sentimentalities.

Before the test also involves creating a positive attitude, so mental preparation should also be a point of concentration. There are many keys to creating a positive attitude. Should fears become rushing in, make a visualization of taking the exam, doing well, and seeing an A written on the paper. Write out a list of affirmations that will bring a feeling of confidence, such as "I am doing well in my English class," "I studied well and know my material," "I enjoy this class." Even if the affirmations aren't believed at first, it sends a positive message to the subconscious which will result in an alteration of the overall belief system, which is the system that creates reality.

If a sensation of panic begins, work with the fear and imagine the very worst! Work through the entire scenario of not passing the test, failing the entire course, and dropping out of school, followed by not getting a job, and pushing a shopping cart through the dark alley where you'll live. This will place things into perspective! Then, practice deep breathing and create a visualization of the opposite situation - achieving an "A" on the exam, passing the entire course, receiving the degree at a graduation ceremony.

On the day of the test, there are many things to be done to ensure the best results, as well as the most calm outlook. The following stages are suggested in order to maximize test-taking potential:

Begin the examination day with a moderate breakfast, and avoid any coffee or beverages with caffeine if the test taker is prone to jitters. Even people who are used to managing caffeine can feel jittery or light-headed when it is taken on a test day.
Attempt to do something that is relaxing before the examination begins. As last minute cramming clouds the mastering of overall concepts, it is better to use this time to create a calming outlook.
Be certain to arrive at the test location well in advance, in order to provide time to select a location that is away from doors, windows and other distractions, as well as giving enough time to relax before the test begins.
Keep away from anxiety generating classmates who will upset the sensation of stability and relaxation that is being attempted before the exam.
Should the waiting period before the exam begins cause anxiety, create a self-distraction by reading a light magazine or something else that is relaxing and simple.

During the exam itself, read the entire exam from beginning to end, and find out how much time should be allotted to each individual problem. Once writing the exam, should more time be taken for a problem, it should be abandoned, in order to begin another problem. If there is time at the end, the unfinished problem can always be returned to and completed.

Read the instructions very carefully - twice - so that unpleasant surprises won't follow during or after the exam has ended.

When writing the exam, pretend that the situation is actually simply the completion of homework within a library, or at home. This will assist in forming a relaxed atmosphere, and will allow the brain extra focus for the complex thinking function.

Begin the exam with all of the questions with which the most confidence is felt. This will build the confidence level regarding the entire exam and will begin a quality momentum. This will also create encouragement for trying the problems where uncertainty resides.

Going with the "gut instinct" is always the way to go when solving a problem. Second guessing should be avoided at all costs. Have confidence in the ability to do well.

For essay questions, create an outline in advance that will keep the mind organized and make certain that all of the points are remembered. For multiple choice, read every answer, even if the correct one has been spotted - a better one may exist.

Continue at a pace that is reasonable and not rushed, in order to be able to work carefully. Provide enough time to go over the answers at the end, to check for small errors that can be corrected.

Should a feeling of panic begin, breathe deeply, and think of the feeling of the body releasing sand through its pores. Visualize a calm, peaceful place, and include all of the sights, sounds and sensations of this image. Continue the deep breathing, and take a few minutes to continue this with closed eyes. When all is well again, return to the test.

If a "blanking" occurs for a certain question, skip it and move on to the next question. There will be time to return to the other question later. Get everything done that can be done, first, to guarantee all the grades that can be compiled, and to build all of the confidence possible. Then return to the weaker questions to build the marks from there.

Remember, one's own reality can be created, so as long as the belief is there, success will follow. And remember: anxiety can happen later, right now, there's an exam to be written!

After the examination is complete, whether there is a feeling for a good grade or a bad grade, don't dwell on the exam, and be certain to follow through on the reward that was promised...and enjoy it! Don't dwell on any mistakes that have been made, as there is nothing that can be done at this point anyway.

Additionally, don't begin to study for the next test right away. Do something relaxing for a while, and let the mind relax and prepare itself to begin absorbing information again.

From the results of the exam - both the grade and the entire experience, be certain to learn from what has gone on. Perfect studying habits and work some more on confidence in order to make the next examination experience even better than the last one.

Learn to avoid places where openings occurred for laziness, procrastination and day dreaming.

Use the time between this exam and the next one to better learn to relax, even learning to relax on cue, so that any anxiety can be controlled during the next exam. Learn how to relax the body. Slouch in your chair if that helps. Tighten and then relax all of the different muscle groups, one group at a time, beginning with the feet and then working all the way up to the neck and face. This will ultimately relax the muscles more than they were to begin with. Learn how to breathe deeply and comfortably, and focus on this breathing going in and out as a relaxing thought. With every exhale, repeat the word "relax."

As common as test anxiety is, it is very possible to overcome it. Make yourself one of the test-takers who overcome this frustrating hindrance.

Special Report: Additional Bonus Material

Due to our efforts to try to keep this book to a manageable length, we've created a link that will give you access to all of your additional bonus material.

Please visit http://www.mometrix.com/bonus948/rtrp to access the information.